CAMBRIDGE LIBRARY COLLECTION

Books of enduring scholarly value

Women's Writing

The later twentieth century saw a huge wave of academic interest in women's writing, which led to the rediscovery of neglected works from a wide range of genres, periods and languages. Many books that were immensely popular and influential in their own day are now studied again, both for their own sake and for what they reveal about the social, political and cultural conditions of their time. A pioneering resource in this area is Orlando: Women's Writing in the British Isles from the Beginnings to the Present (http://orlando.cambridge.org), which provides entries on authors' lives and writing careers, contextual material, timelines, sets of internal links, and bibliographies. Its editors have made a major contribution to the selection of the works reissued in this series within the Cambridge Library Collection, which focuses on non-fiction publications by women on a wide range of subjects from astronomy to biography, music to political economy, and education to prison reform.

A Voyage Round the World, in the *Gorgon* Man of War

In 1791, Mary Ann Parker accompanied her husband, Captain John Parker, on a voyage to deliver supplies to New South Wales. *This book of* 1795 records their travels round the Cape of Good Hope to New South Wales and back, offering valuable insights into late eighteenth-century colonialism, trade, and slavery, as well as the social worlds of Europeans who made careers in the business of empire. Published by subscription following the death of her husband, Parker's travelogue also offers poignant witness to the conditions for women's authorship at the close of the eighteenth century. As she assures her readers, 'nothing but the greatest distress could ever have induced her to solicit beneficence in the manner she has done, for the advantage of her family'. Engaging and observant, Parker's book is an important addition to the canon of early women's travel writing. For more information on this author, see http://orlando.cambridge.org/public/svPeople?person_id=parkma

Cambridge University Press has long been a pioneer in the reissuing of out-of-print titles from its own backlist, producing digital reprints of books that are still sought after by scholars and students but could not be reprinted economically using traditional technology. The Cambridge Library Collection extends this activity to a wider range of books which are still of importance to researchers and professionals, either for the source material they contain, or as landmarks in the history of their academic discipline.

Drawing from the world-renowned collections in the Cambridge University Library, and guided by the advice of experts in each subject area, Cambridge University Press is using state-of-the-art scanning machines in its own Printing House to capture the content of each book selected for inclusion. The files are processed to give a consistently clear, crisp image, and the books finished to the high quality standard for which the Press is recognised around the world. The latest print-on-demand technology ensures that the books will remain available indefinitely, and that orders for single or multiple copies can quickly be supplied.

The Cambridge Library Collection will bring back to life books of enduring scholarly value (including out-of-copyright works originally issued by other publishers) across a wide range of disciplines in the humanities and social sciences and in science and technology.

A Voyage Round the World, in the *Gorgon* Man of War

MARY ANN PARKER

CAMBRIDGE UNIVERSITY PRESS

Cambridge, New York, Melbourne, Madrid, Cape Town, Singapore,
São Paolo, Delhi, Dubai, Tokyo, Mexico City

Published in the United States of America by Cambridge University Press, New York

www.cambridge.org
Information on this title: www.cambridge.org/9781108018883

This edition first published 1795
This digitally printed version 2010

ISBN 978-1-108-01888-3 Paperback

V O Y A G E

ROUND THE

W O R L D,

I N

THE GORGON MAN OF WAR:
Captain JOHN PARKER.

PERFORMED AND WRITTEN BY HIS WIDOW;

FOR THE ADVANTAGE OF A NUMEROUS FAMILY.

DEDICATED, BY PERMISSION,

T O

HER ROYAL HIGHNESS
THE PRINCESS OF WALES.

L O N D O N:

PRINTED BY JOHN NICHOLS, RED-LION-PASSAGE, FLEET-STREET.

AND SOLD BY

Mr. DEBRETT, Piccadilly; Mr. PRIDDEN, No. 100, Fleet-Street;
Messrs. WILKIE, Paternoster-Row; and Mr. RICHARDSON,
at the Royal Exchange. 1795.

TO

HER ROYAL HIGHNESS

THE PRINCESS OF WALES,

WITH GRATEFUL THANKS

FOR HER

CONDESCENDING PERMISSION,

THE FOLLOWING WORK

IS MOST HUMBLY DEDICATED

BY HER ROYAL HIGHNESS'S

MOST DEVOTED,

AND MOST OBEDIENT SERVANT,

MARY ANN PARKER.

No. 6, *Little Chelsea, June* 25, 1795.

PREFACE.

IT having been moſt unjuſtly and injuriouſly reported, that the Authoreſs is worth a conſiderable ſum of money; ſhe thinks it her duty thus publicly to avow, that nothing but the greateſt diſtreſs could ever have induced her to ſolicit beneficence in the manner ſhe has done, for the advantage of her family.

If

If this traducing report originates (and it can no otherwife) from Captain Parker's being entitled to a fhare of prize-money, accruing from fucceffes in the Weft-Indies; fhe has to lament, that his debts are unfortunately too confiderable to give his children one hope of any thing coming to them after they are difcharged.—It is her duty to bring them up not to expect any thing, as it is her firft wifh that the creditors fhould be juftly reimburfed their demands.

The

The unhoped-for fuccefs fhe has met with in Subfcriptions to this publication demands her acknow-ledgements; and fhe trufts her fitua-tion as a nurfe, and being obliged to attend fo much to her domeftic concerns, will be accepted as an apology for the brevity and other greater demerits of the book.

LIST

L I S T

O F

S U B S C R I B E R S.

A.

SIR Jofeph Andrews, Bart. of *Shawe.*
Lieut. Colonel Affleck, 23d Dragoons
Captain John Arbuthnot, Royal Artillery.
Lieut. Anftruther, Royal Navy.
William Arbuthnot, Efq. *Cariacou, Weft Indies.*
George Arbuthnot, Efq. *Navy Pay-Office.*
Robert Arbuthnot, Jun. Efq.
Captain Afkew, Romney Fencibles.
Alexander Adair, Efq. *Pall-Mall.*

S. Alderfey,

S. Alderfey, Efq. *Navy Pay-Office.*

Mr. Edmund Antrobus, *Strand.*

Mr. Jofeph Ainfworth, *Blackburn.*

Mr. William Afpinall, *Ditto.*

Mr. Frederick Accum.

Mr. Richard Atkinfon.

Mr. Thomas Aloes.

Mr. Adams.

B.

Right Hon. Earl of Banbury.

Sir Jofeph Banks, Bart.

Lady Banks.

Colonel Bifhopp, *Knightfbridge.*

Lieut. Col. Braddyll, M.P. R. Lancafhire Militia.

Hon. Major Bridgeman, M. P. Ditto.

Hon. Mrs. Bofcawen, *South Audley-Street.*

Major Byron, late of the 12th Regiment.

Captain Burnett, Bengal Artillery.

Captain Bootle, Royal Lancafhire Militia.

Captain Briftow, Wiltfhire Militia.

Mifs Briftow.

Mr. Briflow.

Captain Robert Burrows, *Francis Eaft-Indiaman.*

Francis Barker, Efq. *Knightfbridge.*

Rev. T. Brown, *Dornfby, Lincolnfhire.*

Nicholas

Nicholas Bond, Efq. *Sloane-Street.*

Richard Barker, Efq. 2d Life Guards.

Robert Barnwell, Efq.

Jeremiah Berry, Efq. *Norfolk.*

John Beddingfield, Efq. *Navy Pay-Office.*

T. D. Bofwell, Efq. *Ditto.*

William Barclay, Efq. *Ditto.*

William Bankes, Efq. *Winftanley.*

David Bull, Efq.

Edward Blair, Efq. *Horkfley.*

Mr. Jofeph Budworth, F. S. A. *Sloane-Street.*

Mrs. Budworth.

Rev. W. Beloe, F. S. A. *James-Street, Weftminfter.*

Mr. George Barke, *Brompton.*

Mr. Edward Bill, *New Bridge-Street.*

Mr. John Berwick, *Pall-Mall.*

Mr. Browell, *Scotland-Yard.*

Mr. Barke, *Knightfbridge.*

Mr. Arthur Brocas, *Francis Eaft-Indiaman.*

Mrs. Brocas.

Mr. J. Bainbridge, jun. *Sloane-Street.*

Mr. Battey, *Ditto.*

Mr. Biffet, *Ditto.*

Mrs. Barley.

Mrs. Bell.

Mifs Blafhfield, *Sloane-Street.*

Mr. John Blackwell.

Mr.

Mr. Biddulph.
Mr. Browne.
Mr. Barlow.
Mr. Blackett.
Mr. Alexander Butler, *Blackburn.*
Mr. Richard Birley, *Ditto.*
Mr. Samuel Bower, *Ditto.*
Mr. Robert Broadbelt, *Ditto.*
Mr. David Bleffett, *Ditto.*
Mrs. Brook, *Ditto.*
Mifs Babington, *Sloane-Street.*
Mrs. Bofquet.
Mr. Thomas Burch.

C.

Right Hon. Lord Compton.
Admiral Sir Roger Curtis.
Colonel J. F. Cradock.
Major Clayton, *Wigan.*
Captain Chefshyre, Royal Navy.
Captain Crooke, Royal Lancafhire Militia.
Captain Chriftian, Royal Navy.
Lieutenant Clotwyk, South Hants Militia.
Richard Cardwell, Efq. *Blackburn.*
Richard Cardwell, Jun. Efq. *Ditto.*

Henry

Henry Cranftoun, Efq. *Navy Pay-Office.*
Chriftopher Cook, Efq. *Ditto.*
John Church, Efq. *Ditto.*
S. Child, Efq. *Ditto.*
William Creffwell, Efq. *Ditto.*
John Clarke, Efq. *Knightfbridge.*
Thomas Carter, Efq. *Sloane-Street.*
Richard Henry Croft, Efq. *Pall-Mall.*
George Cloake, Efq. *Turnham-Green.*
William Cowan, Efq.
Mr. William Clofe, *Pall-Mall.*
Mifs Cocks, *Sloane-Street.*
Mr. P. Cooper, *Arundel-Street.*
Mr. Carrol, *Sloane-Street.*
Mr. Codd, *Hans-Place.*
Mr Charles Cullen.
Mr. Capel.
Mr. Chalmers.

D.

Colonel Delhofte, R. M. V.
Captain Drummond, *Knightfbridge.*
Captain Darby.
John Davies, Efq. *Navy Pay-Office.*
Richard Draper, Efq. *Ditto.*

Mr.

Mr. R. Dolton, at Mr. Glover's, *Knightfbridge.*
Mr. James Dewar, *Clement's Inn.*
Mr. Thomas Docker, Surgeon in the Army.
Mr. Jofeph Docker, *Pall-Mall.*
Mr. H. H. Deacon, *Sloane-Street.*
Mr. William Dawes, *Fenchurch-Street.*
Mr. Thomas Dowding.
Mr. Douglas.
Mr. Dunell.

F.

Major John Edwards.

F.

Sir James Foulis, Bart.
Captain Frith, North Hants Militia.
George Fennell, Efq. *Navy Pay-Office.*
T. Fitzgerald, Efq. *Ditto.*
Edward Bofcawen Frederick, Efq. *Berkeley-Square.*
C. W. Flint, Efq.
Samuel Felton, Efq. F. R. S.
E. Foulker, Efq.
James Fallowfield, Efq.
John Fofter, Efq.
Rev. Mr. Ferrers, *Bath.*

Mifs

Mifs Fernfide.
Mrs. Fowden, *Wigan.*
Mr. Henry Fielden, *Blackburn.*
Mr. John Fielden, *Ditto.*
Mr. William Fielden, *Ditto.*

G.

Capt. Lord Vifcount Garlies, Royal Navy.
Sir Nigel Bowyer Grefley, Bart.
Colonel Gledftanes.
Mrs. Gledftanes.
Lieutenant Colonel Henry Grey.
Major Thomas Grey.
Captain William Grey.
Captain George Grey, Royal Navy.
Major Grymes, *Sloane-Street.*
Captain Grueber, *Ditto.*
Captain Gage.
Captain Gillam, Madras Infantry.
William Gillam, Efq.
G. J. Gafcoigne, Efq. *Navy Pay-Office.*
J. Glover, Efq. *Jobbing's Buildings, Knightfbridge.*
Rev J. Gamble, *Knightfbridge*
Lieutenant John Gardiner, Royal Navy.

William

[xvi]

William Gardiner, Efq.
Jafper Leigh Goodwin, Efq.
William Grefley, Efq. *Twickenham.*
Thomas Gardnor, Efq. *Upper Grofvenor-Street.*
Rev. Mr. Gamman, *Cheapfide.*
Mrs. Gines.
Mrs. Grefley.
Mr. Thomas Gill.
Mr. Goldney.
Mr. John Grant, *Cockfpur-Street.*
Mr. Ifaac Glover, *Blackburn.*
Mr. Green, *Dartford.*
Mr. Robert Gray.
Mr. Gray.
Mrs. Gray.

H.

Right Hon. Lady Caroline Herbert.
Charles Herbert, Efq.
Honorable Lady Honeywood.
Colonel Stephens Howe, *Aid de Camp to His Majefty.*
Colonel Henderfon.
Colonel Otho Hamilton, *James Street, Weftminfter.*
Captain Hamilton, 3d Life Guards, *Ditto.*
Captain Howarth.
Dr. Harrington, M. D. *Bath.*

7   Captain

Captain Hopwood, Royal Lancashire Militia.

Lieut. Thomas Hitchbone, late of 12th Reg.

D. Harmood, Esq. *Navy Pay-Office.*

William Hutton, Esq. *Ditto.*

Alexander Hislop, Esq. *Ditto.*

William Hamerton, Esq.

William Higden, Esq.

John Hale, Esq.

John Fowden Hindle, Esq. *Blackburn.*

Hugh Robert Hughes, Esq. *Pall-Mall.*

Rev. E. Harris, *Sloane-Street.*

Mrs. Harris.

Miss Harris.

Miss Sophia Harris.

Rev. Mr. Harrison, *Brompton.*

Rev. James Holme, Vicar of *Shap, Westmorland.*

Miss Catherine Hunter,, *Adelphi.*

Mr. Thomas Hollis, *Park-Place, Knightsbridge.*

Mr. Peyton Hadley.

Mr. Howison, *Hammersmith.*

Mrs. Holland, *Hans Town.*

Miss Holland.

Mr. Holme, *Thames-Street.*

Mrs. Hockley, *Blacklands.*

Mr. Harding.

Mr. Ham.

John Hull, M. D. *Blackburn.*

b   Mr.

Mr. William Hornby, *Blackburn.*
Mr. John Hornby, *Ditto.*
Mr. Hicks.

J.

Captain Jekyll, 43d Regiment.
George Jeffries, Efq. *Sloane-Street.*
George Jeffries, Efq. Jun.
Mr. Jackfon, *Knightfbridge.*
Mrs. Jackfon.
Mrs. Jarvis.
Mr. Johnfton.

K.

Mr. Kelly, *Sloane-Strcet.*
Mrs. Kearfley, *Wigan.*

L.

Captain Sir Wilfred Lawfon, Bart. R. L. M.
Lady Lawfon.
Captain Lyons, 11th Dragoons.

Mrs.

N.

Enſign Neville, 3d Guards.
—— Norris, Eſq.
J. Neſbitt, Eſq. M. P.
William Newton, Eſq. *Sloane-Street.*
Mr. John Neville, *Blackburn.*
Rev. R. Nares, F.S.A. *James-Street, Weſtminſter.*
Mr. John Noble, *Fleet-Street.*
Mr. William Noble, *Pall-Mall.*
Mr. Deputy Nichols.
Miſs Nichols.
Mr. John-Bowyer Nichols.
Mr. Naylor, *Mile End.*

O.

Rev. George Ogle.
Mrs. Orrell.
Mr. Thomas Oldfield, *Union-Street.*

P. Viſcounteſs

Mrs. Lyons.
Captain Lane, *Sloane-Street.*
Captain John Larkins, *Greenwich.*
Lieut. Lutwidge, R. Lancafhire Militia.
Library *at Bampton Vicarage, Weftmorland.*
William Lockhart, Efq. *Navy Pay-Office.*
—— Lewis, Efq.
Mifs Eliz. Locker, *Greenwich.*
Mr. Ralph Lattic, *Blackburn.*
Mr. John Livefay, *Ditto.*
Mr. Lonquet.
Mr. Long, *Upper Brook Street.*
Mr. Henry Longbottam, *Borough.*

M.

Sir John Miller, Bart.
General Melvill.
Honourable Captain Murray, Royal Navy.
Captain Richard Morrice, Ditto.
Captain Simon Miller, Ditto.
Captain Maude, Ditto.
Mrs. Maude.
Captain Machell, R. Lancafhire Militia.
Dr. Moore.
Mifs Hannah More, *Bath.*
Thomas Maberley, Efq.

Thomas

Thomas Maude, Efq. *Downing-Street.*

Henry Grey Mainall, Efq. M. D.

Samuel Maſkall, Efq.

John Minyer, Efq.

D. Minors, Jun. Efq.

Miſs Merry.

Mr. Maſh, *St. James's Palace.*

Miſs Murray, *Clarges-Street.*

Rev. James Mac Quhoe, *Blackburn.*

Mr. William Miller, *Bond Street.*

Mr. John Marſhall, *Aldermary Church-Yard.*

Mrs. Marſhall.

Mr. Michie, *Sloane-Street.*

Mr. William Maude, Royal Navy.

Miſs Milles.

Mr. Mills.

Mr. Maundrill, *Knightſbridge.*

Mr. Maundrill, Jun.

Mrs. Middleditch.

Mr. Donald Maclean, *Blackburn.*

Mr. Bertie Markland, *Ditto.*

Mr. Charles Morgan, *Ditto.*

N. Enſign

P.

Vifcountefs Palmerfton.
N. Pierce, Efq. *Navy Pay-Office.*
C. Purvis, Efq. *Ditto.*
G. Player, Efq. *Ditto.*
Roger Palmer, Efq. *Oxford-Street.*
Francis Palmer, Efq. *Sloane-Street.*
William Pollock, Efq.
Jofeph Potter, Efq. *Chelfea.*
Charles Phillips, Efq.
Thomas Poole, Efq.
Captain Parker, 11th Light Dragoons.
Rev. John Pridden, M. A. F. S. A.
Mifs Phillips, *Sloane-Street.*
Mr. William Parrys, *Knightfbridge.*
Mr. Plafkett.
Mr. James de la Pryme, *Blackburn.*
Mr. John Parkhoufe.
Mr. Peyton, *Navy-Office.*
Mr. Edward Powell.
Mr. Palmer, *St. James's Street.*
Mrs. Pocock.
Mr. Pettiwood.

Mr.

Mr. Parsons.
Mr. J. Plumridge, *Sloane-Street.*
Mr. Charles Pincent, *Edward-Street.*
Mr. Edward Powell.
Mr. G. Puffer, *Knightsbridge.*

R.

General Rainsford.
Mrs. Rainsford.
Captain Edward Ridgway, R. Lancashire Militia.
Lieutenant Radford, Ditto.
Kemys Radcliffe, Esq. *Navy Pay-Office.*
Walter Reed, Esq. *Ditto.*
George Rofs, Esq. *Duke-Street, Adelphi.*
Major Andrew Rofs, *Ditto.*
William Roberts, Esq.
John Reid, Esq.
Rev. Dr. Reynett, *Prescott-Street.*
Mrs. Reynett.
Mr. J. A. Rucker, *Sloane-Street.*
Mrs. Ruffell.
Mr. Rieman.
Chevalier Rufpini, *Pall-Mall.*
Mr. Ramfay Robinfon, *Kenfington.*
Mr. Thomas Richardfon.

Mrs.

Mrs. Ricketts, *Lower Seymour-Street.*
Mr. William Rothwell, *Sloane-Street.*
Mr. Randoll.

S.

Right Honourable the Earl of Scarborough.
Colonel Hans Sloane, M. P. *Upper Harley-Street.*
Lieut. Colonel William Skerrett.
Major Smith, Royal Artillery.
Captain Squires, Royal Navy.
Captain John Schank, Ditto.
Captain Skinner.
Dr. Shufan, *New Bridge-Street.*
Mrs. Stephens, *Adelphi.*
Mifs Stevens.
George Swaffield, Efq. *Navy Pay-Office.*
John Swaffield, Efq. *Ditto.*
James Slade, Efq. *Ditto.*
Henry Slade, Efq. *Ditto.*
Walter Stirling, Efq. *Ditto.*
Thomas Sermon, Efq.
Walter Stott, Efq. *Liverpool.*
Henry Sudell, Efq. *Blackburn.*
Samuel Swinton, Efq. *Sloane Street.*
Alexander Scott, Efq.

William

William Smith, Jun. Efq. *Lombard-Street.*

James Symes, Efq.

Robert Saunders, Efq. *Southend, Kent.*

Rev. Mr. Symes.

Edward Gray Saunders, Efq. *Oxford-Street.*

Rev. Thomas Staikie, M. A. Vicar of *Blackburn.*

Edward Stuart, Efq.

Mr. Sealey.

Mr. Seaman, *Strand.*

Mr. Thomas Somers.

Mrs. Saunders, *Sloane-Street.*

O. B. Smyth, M. D.

Mr. Henry Stacie, late Soldier 58th Regiment.

Mrs. Smith, *Woodstock.*

Mrs. Sones.

Mrs. Stuart.

Mrs. Shepherd, *Kelvedon.*

Mrs. Seaten, *Suffolk-Street.*

Mrs. Shricol, *Westham.*

T.

Admiral Charles Thompfon.

Captain Thornton, Royal Artillery.

Captain Thomas, 11th Light Dragoons.

Captain Trotty, Royal Navy.

Captain Taylor, *Carteret Packet.*

Alexander

Alexander Trotter, Efq. *Navy Pay-Office.*
William Taylor, Efq. *Ditto.*
William Taylor, Jun. Efq. *Ditto.*
Adam Thomfon, Efq. *Ditto.*
Mr. Charles Tweidie, *Ditto.*
Charles Tweedie, Jun. Efq. *Ditto.*
Rev. Dr. John Trotter, *Hans Square.*
John Turing, Efq. *Sloane Street.*
Mrs. Turing.
Mifs Turing.
William Thompfon, LL.D.
John Thoyts, Efq. *Merton.*
Rev. Mr. Thomas, *Strand.*
Mr. Thomas Turner, *Blackburn.*
Mifs Travers, *Ditto.*
Mr. Thomas Thompfon, *Caftle-Street.*
Mr. F. Trecourt, *Sloane-Street.*
Mr. John Townfend.
Mr. Richard Twifs.
Mr. Toulmin.

U.

Capt. Vefey, 39th Regiment.
Lieut. Upton, R. Lancafhire Militia.
G. Urquhart, *Navy Pay-Office.*
Mr. Virtue, *Hammerfmith.*

W. Major

W.

Major Wathen.

Captain Charles White, Royal Navy.

Captain Williamfon, Royal Lancafhire.

Captain Wright, 99th Regiment.

Thomas Wilfon, Efq. *Navy Pay-Office*.

Thomas Walker, Efq. *Ditto*.

Mr. William Ward, *Ditto*.

William Webb, Efq. *Conduit-Street*.

William Walter, Efq. *New Bridge-Street*.

Thomas Watfan, Efq.

—— Walker, Efq.

J. Warner, Efq. *Knightfbridge*.

Jekyll Wyatt, Efq.

Thomas Watfon, Efq.

Mrs. Wallace, *Sloane-Street*.

Mr. Wilmot, *Thornhaugh-Street*.

Mr. Watkins.

Mrs. Welcher, *Sloane-Street*.

Mifs Welcher.

Mr. Richard White, *Piccadilly*.

Mr. John Wright, *Old Bond-Street*.

Mifs White, *Bath*.

Mr. William Ware, *Sloane-Street*.

Mr. White.

Mr. Richard Wimburn.

Mr. Wagner, *Pall-Mall*.

C O N-

CONTENTS.

CHAP. I.

CHAP. II.

CHAP.

C H A P. III.

C H A P. IV.

C H A P. V.

CHAP.

CHAP. VI.

CHAP. VII.

CHAP. VIII.

CHAP.

C H A P. IX.

C H A P. X.

C H A P. XI.

C H A P. XII.

A VOYAGE

NARRATIVE

OF A

VOYAGE ROUND THE WORLD.

CHAP. I.

*Reasons for undertaking the voyage—
set out for Portsmouth—passengers
on board--sail from Spithead—arrive at the island of Teneriffe—
pay a visit to the Governor—description of the town of Santa Cruz—an
excursion to Puerto Oratava—a
laughable occurrence — Lieutenant*

B   *Rye—*

*Rye—another excurſion—return to
the ſhip—and ſet ſail.*

ON the *firſt* day of January **1791,**
my late husband, Captain John
Parker, was appointed by the Right
Honourable the Lords Commiſſioners
of the Admiralty to the command of
His Majeſty's ſhip the Gorgon —On
the *ſecond* he received his commiſſion.
The ſhip was then lying at her moor-
ings off Common-hand in Portſ-
mouth harbour, refitting for her intended voyage to New South Wales,
and exchanging the proviſions ſhe
then had, for the neweſt and beſt in
ſtore.

There were embarked for their
paſſage to the aforenamed colony, a

part

part of the new corps that had been raifed for that place, commanded by Major Grofe. By the laft day of January the fhip was ready for fea; and on the *firft* day of February the pilot came on board, in order to conduct her out of the harbour to Spithead.

When things were in this ftate of forwardnefs, it was propofed to me to accompany Captain Parker in the intended expedition to New Holland. A fortnight was allowed me for my decifion. An indulgent husband waited my anfwer at Portfmouth: I did not therefore take a minute's confideration; but, by return of poft, forwarded one perfectly confonant to his requeft, and my moft fanguine wifhes—that of going with *him* to

the remoteſt parts of the globe; although my conſiderate readers will
naturally ſuppoſe that my feelings were
ſomewhat wounded at the thoughts
of being ſo long abſent from two
dear children, and a mother, with
whom I had travelled into France,
Italy, and Spain; and from whom I
had never been ſeparated a fortnight
at one time during the whole courſe
of my life.

Attended by an intimate friend, I
repaired to the Weſt end of the town,
and ſet off for Portſmoutn the next
morning. We remained at Spithead
until the 12th of March. In the in-
terim orders had arrived to receive
on board Captain Gidley King, of the
Royal Navy, the intended Lieutenant
Governor

Governor of Norfolk Ifland in the Pacific Ocean, together with Mrs. King and their family ; alfo to dif-embark Major Grofe, and fuch part of the corps as were on board, except Mr. Burton a botanift, Mr. Baines the chaplain, and Mr. Grimes, who, with their attendants, were directed to be continued on board, and to take their paffage for the new fettlement.

On Tuefday, the 15th of March, we failed from Spithead, by way of St. Helens; and, after a fortnight's feafoning and buffeting in the chan-nel, I began to enjoy the voyage I had undertaken ; and with the polite attention of the officers on board, and my amiable companion Mrs. King, we glided over many a watery grave

B 3   with

with peace of mind, and uninterrupt-
ed happinefs; although many calms
tended to render our paffage to the
ifland of *Teneriffe* fomewhat tedious.

We arrived, however, fafe in the
bay of *Santa Cruz* on the *fifteenth* of
April; and captain Parker fent the
fecond lieutenant on fhore, to acquaint
the Governor of our having put into
that port for refrefhment, and offered to exchange falutes, provided
his Excellency would affure him the
return of an equal number of guns
from the garrifon; at the fame time
informing him that he fhould have
the honour, together with the officers, of waiting on him the enfuing
day; and that lieutenant governor
King of Norfolk Ifland was a paf-
fenger,

fenger, and alfo intended to do himfelf the honour of paying his refpects
to his Excellency.

The officer returned with the Governor's anfwer, that whatever the
fhip ftood in need of, fhe might have;
and that an officer fhould be fent on-
board, to fignify the time when it
would be moft convenient for His Excellency to receive the compliments
we had been fo polite as to offer, of
waiting on him; but that he had
orders from his Court not to return
any falute to a foreign Ship of War.

About half an hour after the return
of the officer, one of the Governor's
Aid-de-Camps came on board: he
congratulated us, in his Excellency's

name, on our safe arrival, and informed us that the Governor would
be happy to fee us, and requefted that
we would favour him with our company to dine with him on the enfuing
day.

The invitation was accepted. Our
party confifted of Lieutenant Governor King, his lady, our officers, together with Mr. Grimes, and Mr.
Baines. The company at Don An-
tonio di Gutierez (that was the name
of the Governor) were; the former
Governor the Marquis di Branciforti,
the Lieutenant Governor and his
lady, with feveral other officers and
their ladies.

The reception we met with, and particularly the compliments *di los ma-*
nos,

nos*, would have ſtruck me by their
ſingularity, had I not reſided when
very young upwards of three years
in Spain; during which time I had
every reaſon to believe them particularly attentive to the *Engliſh ladies:*
and I hope it will be allowed me to
remark the great ſatisfaction which
they expreſſed at my being capable
of converſing in their own language—
a pleaſure which I could not help
participating with them, from having
it in my power to be of ſome. ſer-
vice, as *Interpreter General* to the party with whom I had the ſatisfaction of
ſailing.

* A compliment paid in Spain by the ladies to
each other on entering a room. The laſt comer
juſt touches the hand of every lady, at the ſame
time curtſeying and repeating continually " *di los*
" *manos.*"

It

It being Paffion-week, the dinner, although fumptuous, confifted of many difhes dreffed with oil.—After having, from hunger and politenefs, ate more than we wifhed of the leaft rancid difhes, not expecting any plain ones to make their appearance; we were quite furprized when a large roafted Turkey, dreffed quite in the Englifh fafhion, was brought on the table:—had it made an earlier entrance, it would have been well finifhed, but, unfortunately, it came fo unexpectedly, that our appetites had been fatisfied, with a previous courfe of rancid plenty.

After dinner our formidable party paraded the town, which I fuppofe to be very near a mile in length, and about

about half a mile in breadth. There
are feveral neat churches in it, but
only one good ftreet, which is remarkably broad :—the reft are generally very narrow, and abound in beg-
gars, who are extremely troublefome
to travellers.

At fun-fet we returned on board,
well fatisfied with the reception we
had met with ; and on the following
day, the fame party dined at Mr.
Rooney's, a Gentleman in partnerfhip
with the Englifh houfe of Meff. Little
and Co. and to whom Captain Parker had been introduced by means of
a letter from Sir Andrew Hammond.
From a defire of making me acquainted with fome Spanifh ladies, Mr.
Rooney engaged us in an afternoon's
walk

walk to visit Captain Adams, the
Captain of the Port, and there I had
the pleasure of meeting with several
females. They seemed highly de-
lighted with my hat and dress, and
took singular satisfaction in repeatedly
taking off the former, and in examin-
ing my coat, which was half uniform.
My having formerly travelled in Spain,
and consequently having acquired a
tolerable knowledge of their language
procured me unusual attention, such
as I shall ever remember with pleasure, though mingled with a degree
of regret, arising from the improba-
bility of my ever revisiting a country,
in which I had the happiness to meet
with unlimited kindness.

The next morning we were pre-
sented with sallads, fruits, lemons,
&c.

&c. from different inhabitants of the town, who feemed to vie with each other in prefenting us with thofe falutary refrefhments.

The following day was fixed for an excurfion to *Puerto Oratava*. Accompanied by Governor King, his lady, our firft Lieutenant, and a young gentleman belonging to Meff. Little and Co. we went on fhore at day-break, and after breakfafting mounted our buricos or donkeys. The roads (hardly deferving that appellation) were rugged indeed ; in fome places the ftones were fufficiently out of the ground to afford us feats, but the good humour which reigned amongft our party made ample amends for any trifling difficulty of that nature—and

indeed

indeed little difficulties make focial excurfions more interefting.

Our firft halting-place was a fmall hut, where Mr. Malcolme, a gentle-man belonging to the fame houfe, had taken care to provide us with bifcuits, wine, &c. Having refrefhed ourfelves we continued our ride un-til *meridian,* when it was judged pru-dent for us to tarry during the heat of the day. Here Mr. Malcolme had alfo procured a cold collation, or a firft dinner.——Two fultry hours hav-ing paffed away very cheerfully, we again mounted our buricos, and, upon my making ufe of the Spanifh method of quickening their pace, my animal fet off on full fpeed, left the muleteer ftaring with aftonifhment, and poor

me

me rolling down a fteep hill; but perceiving the party, who had not got up with us, coming rapidly to my affiftance, fearful left they fhould gallop over me, I arofe as quickly as poffible, and fcrambling to a ftone fat myfelf down upon it, and laughed as heartily as I ever recollected to have done in my life. This little accident let my muleteer into the fecret of my having underftood the chief of his converfation with the other, who had the honour of attending my companion Mrs. King, which was " his inclination to ftop at all the *po-fadoes*, or public houfes, we had paffed by."

At a fhort diftance from this laughable fcene, we were met by Mr. Lit-

I   tle,

tle, who very politely conducted us to his town refidence, where he had prepared a moft fplendid entertainment replete with every delicacy of the feafon. The fruits and vegetables were luxuries indeed to us, who had been accuftomed to little choice during our paffage.

From this town, on the fame evening, one of our officers, Lieutenant Rye, accompanied by Mr. Burton the botanift, took his departure for the Peak of Teneriffe, in which enterprize, notwithftanding the great danger pointed out to him at that feafon of the year, he was fortunate enough to fucceed, and arrived at its fummit.

On his return to England, his excurfion was publifhed; and I recommend

mend it to the perufal of my readers; yet muſt at the ſame time take the liberty of obſerving, that although he has been minute as to particulars that tend to the information and benefit of ſuch as may hereafter wiſh to viſit the Peak, he has been too diffident in mentioning the extreme fatigues and difficulties which he underwent in the accompliſhment of his wiſhes. The inhabitants ſpoke of his courage in terms of aſtoniſhment—too much cannot be ſaid in praiſe of his perſeverance, it is ſufficient of itſelf to convince us that no difficulties are inſuperable to the prudent and brave, and at the ſame time brings to my remembrance the following lines of Mr. Rowe :

C   " The

[18]

" The wife and prudent conquer difficulties
" By daring to attempt them : Sloth and folly
" Shiver and fhrink at fight of toil and hazard,
" And make th' impoffibility they fear."

We were the next morning regaled
with a breakfaft equally profufe and
delicate as the preceding meals. The
greater part of that day being too
fultry to walk, we were much in-
debted to the polite and refpectful attention of the aforementioned gentlemen, who, ftudying our amufement, propofed an evening excurfion
to their country refidence, fituated at
a fhort diftance from the town. It
is a fmall neat houfe, ftanding upon a
hill, commanding an extenfive view
of the Bay of Santa-Cruz; the garden is enclofed with myrtle hedges,
the walks were fhaded with vines,
and

and lofty lemon trees, and the par-
terre before the door arranged
with pots of moſt beautiful carna-
tions.

Having comfortably regaled ourſelves, we returned back to tea and
ſupper; retired early, and aroſe at
four the next morning. After break-
faſting we ſet out upon our return;
at *eleven* we ſtopped to partake of
ſome refreſhments, and then proceeded *two* leagues farther, when we again
alighted to avoid the intenſe heat;
during which time Mrs. King and
myſelf ſtrolled to ſeveral little huts.
The inhabitants were ſurprized at ſee-
ing ſtrangers of our ſex alone; but
their aſtoniſhment ſoon ſubſided when
I ſpoke a few words to them in Spa-

C 2   niſh;

niſh ;—from this moment pleaſure was viſible in every countenance ; in proof of which, although their ſpot of ground was ſmall, their kindneſs induced them to preſent us with ſome ſage, and an egg apiece—the *little* all they had to proffer us; and I make no doubt but we were remembered by them the remainder of the day ; nay I will even think they have not yet forgotten us.

Returning to our party, and finding all ready, we remounted, and after riding a few miles our Engliſh friends took leave of us. Their uniform attention has induced me to name them ſo often in this narrative— the only return I ſhall ever have it in my power to make them.

It

[21]

It may afford a fmile to my readers to add, that, after it was found out that I could fpeak Spanifh, I entered into converfation with my muleteer, which made him fo proud of his charge, that, previous to our entering any town or village, he, with great form, requefted me to fit upright, and then fpread my hair very curioufly over my fhoulders.——Poor fellow ! could I be difpleafed with his requeft; fince it arofe, without doubt, from a defire of making me appear to the greateft advantage ?

Thus, by the favour of a ferene evening, we returned to Mr. Rooney's, who wifhed us to fleep on fhore, as the wind began to blow frefh, and

C 3 the

the furf rendered it very unpleafant for us to go on-board; but having refolved prior to my leaving England, to bear every difficulty, if poffible, and determined to ftart none, I, with my good friends, took leave; and, after a few lifts over a heavy fea, we reached the wifhed-for veffel.

The next morning we paid a vifit to the Spanifh Lieutenant Governor's Lady, who introduced us to feveral ladies. The following day Mr. Rooney and Mr. Malcolme favoured us with their company on-board. After dinner they took leave of us, and fhortly after we received from them a prefent of fome lemons, and fuch other fruit as they deemed moft acceptable for our intended voyage.

On

On the 24th of April we attempted
to fail; but unfortunately the anchor
of our veffel hooked the cable of a
Spanifh brig, owing to a ftrong tide;
which broke the window, and carried
away part of our quarter gallery. This
accident detained us until the following day, when we failed with a frefh
and favourable breeze, and faw the
Peak many leagues diftant.

CHAP.

CHAP. II.

*Ceremony of croffing the Equator—ar-
rive at St. Jago—defcription of the
Portugueze inhabitants—a violent
gale—fee the ifland of Saint Trinidad—a defcription of that ifland—
arrive at Simon's Bay—fet out for
the Cape.*

ON the 27th of April we got into
the Trade-Winds. On the 29th we
croffed the line, and paid the ufual
forfeit to Amphitrite and Neptune.
Thofe failors who had croffed the
line before burlefqued the new-com-
ers as much as poffible, calling themfelves Neptune and Amphytrite with
their

their aquatic attendants. They have
the privilege to make themfelves
merry ; and thofe who have never
been in South latitudes purchafe their
freedom by a fmall quantity of liquor.
But the failor or foldier who has none
to give is the objeʧ of their mirth ;
and, the more reftive he is, the more
keen they are to proceed to bufinefs.
A large tub of falt water, with a feat
over it, is placed in the fore-part of
the ſhip, on which the new comer is
reluʧantly put—the feat is drawn
from under him ; and, when rifing
from the tub, feveral pails of water
are thrown over him—he is then
puſhed forward amongſt his laughing
ſhipmates, and is as bufy as the reft
to get others in the fame predica-
ment.

The

The *firſt* of May we expected to
make the iſland of *Sal*—ſaw many
porpoiſes, and, having had moderate
breezes, arrived at *St. Jago* on the
third. Being adviſed not to go on
ſhore, we waited till we had procured abundance of all kinds of refreſhments; in particular, fruit, poul-
try, and goats; all of which articles
were very ſcarce at Teneriffe, owing
to its being ſo early in the Spring.
The turkeys upon this iſland are remarkably fine, and would do credit
to the plumpeſt that Norfolk could
produce.

The ſhips then in Port Praya Bay
were The Phœnix and Lord Camden
Eaſt Indiamen; and, during our ſhort
ſtay,

ftay, The Dutton, Albemarle, Barrington, and Active tranfports, arrived. Here we had the pleafure of
becoming acquainted with Captain
Patterfon, of the New South Wales
corps, and his Lady. We treated
ourfelves with cocoa-nuts and pine-
apples, of which there are great
abundance in this ifland. The Portugueze inhabitants have chiefly been
defaulters in their native country;
and the fallownefs of their com-
plexions proves what a fickly climate
they have to buffet with. The black
inhabitants are robuft, and much inclined, like their mafters, to take advantage of ftrangers; nay, I have
been credibly informed, that they
make no ceremony of cheating one
another, whenever a fuitable opportunity

tunity occurs. They are fond of old cloaths in their exchange for fruit, &c. and a fhabby fuit of old black is efteemed twice as valuable as any other colour.

We left this ifland on the 6th of May—had frefh breezes and violent heat until the 10th. Many fharks were caught, and the tails of the youngeft of them eaten by the men : porpoifes were feen rolling about with great force all around us.

We experienced much heat between the trade-winds, until the 19th, when, for a change, we were overtaken by a moft violent fquall of wind, attended with thunder, lightning, and rain, and the fhip pitched very much. The

The greateſt inconvenience I ſuf-
fered from theſe ſqualls was the neceſſity we were under of having in
the dead lights, which are ſtrong
ſhutters wedged in to prevent a following ſea from breaking into the
ſhip. The noiſe made by the work-
ing of the veſſel, and the ſwinging
of the glaſs ſhades that held our lights,
rendered the cabin very diſmal.

This ſqually weather continued,
with little variation, until the 23d,
when we ſpoke with a French ſhip,
bound to Port L'Orient. They had
nothing to diſpoſe of; but ſent us a
fine turtle, which was a great treat
to thoſe who were fond of the variety
of good food it contains.

On

On the 29th we faw the ifland of
Saint Trinidad, which appears a very
beautiful little fpot : Captain D'Au-
vergne, in a cutter belonging to Com-
modore Johnftone's fleet, was caft
away here. I am told they made
themfelves quite comfortable, as they
faved great part of their ftores ; and,
having fome garden feeds, they grew
up quickly, and cabbages thrived particularly well. This ifland is about
nine miles in circumference, well
wooded, and watered with fertile valleys ; and the Englifh colony, who
were the only inhabitants, left it with
regret. We faw a great quantity of
birds hovering all around; and, as
they are not often difturbed by man,
they range in native freedom. The

2   fea-

fea-birds have plenty of food, from the variety of fifh, particularly the Flying-fifh which is conftantly tormented both by Bonetas and Dolphins, and the birds darting upon them, in their flying efforts to efcape.

On the 30th the weather was very fqually, and the fea rough. We faw pintado-birds, and others ufual in thefe latitudes ; alfo Mother Cary's Chickens—fmall birds, that fly very faft, and are not unlike the fwallow : they are feldom feen but in rough weather ; and failors fay they are the attendants upon ftorms—of courfe they are not partial to them.

This

This weather continued feveral days ; once we were obliged, on account of the roughnefs of the fea, to dine on the deck in the cabin ; but thefe little difficulties were fcarcely felt, the party being in good humour, and our fpirits well fupported by good broth, roaft pig, and plumb-puddings—thanks to my caterer, who had fo well provided for fo long a voyage.

With little variation, we failed till the 19th of June, when land was once more in fight. At ten the next morning the *Bellows Rock* opened to view ; and on the 21ft, at *four* in the afternoon, we arrived, at *Simon's Bay* ; this being the Bay where fhips gene-rally

rally lay during the winter-feafon, as the fudden hurricanes, which fweep round the mountains at tnis period, make the Bay at Cape town too dangerous to rifk a veffel at.

An officer was fent on fhore, to inform the Commandant of our having put in for refrefhment : he fhortly returned, and brought us word, that every thing wanted fhould be readily fupplied; and the next morning the Commandant paid us a vifit on board.

Governor King alfo wrote to Mr. Peter de Witt, a merchant at the Cape of Good Hope ; in confequence of which he waited upon us, and brought with him two carriages to conduct us to the Cape ; the one a

D   chaife,

chaife, drawn by four, the other a kind of waggon, drawn by eight horfes.

On the 23d, eager for a little fhore amufement, we rofe early, and, after breakfafting upon rolls, and fuch fruit as we had procured from the Bay, Lieutenant Governor King, Mrs. King, our firft Lieutenant, Captain Parker, and myfelf, went on fhore—the fort faluting with fifteen guns, and our fhip returning the compliment with an equal number.

CHAP.

CHAP. III.

Set off for Cape Town—ſtop at Falſe-
bay—meet a party of Soldiers—re-
flections—arrive at the Cape—Mrs.
De Witt—ſhipwreck of the Guar-
dian—Lieutenant Riou—a Cape-
breakfaſt—obſervations on the town
and its inhabitants.

I COULD not help being well-
pleaſed at finding myſelf once more
ſafe landed. We loitered ſome time
at Mr. Brank's, where we met Colonel Burrington, of the Bengal army,
who was then at the Cape, for the
re-eſtabliſhment of his health. In a

ſhort

fhort time we fet off for Cape Town, Captain King and Mr. De Witt in the chaife and four, and the reft of us in the carriage drawn with eight horfes, fomewhat refembling a covered waggon, except having feats within, and little gaudy decorations.

The road was exceffively bad, and the carriage not being hung with fprings rendered travelling moft joltingly difagreeable. After having rode about eight or nine miles, we arrived at a houfe fituated in the bottom of *Falfe Bay*, called *Muffleburg:* this houfe, when firft built, was intended by the Governor and Council, as a temporary refidence, being fituated in a good fifhing neighbourhood, and as a place of refrefhment to travellers

travellers paffing to and from Cape-
Town and Simon's Bay.—After the
jolting of our vehicle, we had reafon
to think it a place of relief; and when
we arrived there, we found feveral
officers, with their wives and children, at dinner. We had alfo met
feveral different parties of foldiers
on the road; upon enquiry, we found
it was a regiment marching to Simon's
Bay, in order to be embarked on-
board a Dutch Indiaman bound to Batavia; there having been recently at
that place a great mortality amongft
all claffes of Europeans, faid to be
caufed by the Malays, the natives of
Java, having poifoned the waters.

In relating this circumftance, I cannot but feel myfelf deeply affected, as

D 3   it

it brings to my mind the recollection
of fimilar embarkations that have
lately taken place for thofe cruel
iflands, where fo many brave men
have fallen victims to that worft of
all diftempers, the Yellow Fever—a
diftemper, the fatal effects of which I
have fo heavily experienced, as it has
deprived me of a beloved hufband, the
tender partner of my life, and my
only fupport in the time of trouble
and affliction. When I reflect on his
many virtues, and on the irreparable
lofs which I have unexpectedly fuf-
tained, I cannot help faying, with
General Draper, on a fimilar occafion :

" Why to fuch worth was no duration given ?
" Becaufe perfection is the choice of Heaven."

But

But to proceed—During our ride, we noticed fome remarkable fmall birds with beautiful plumage; but which are not known to fing: their chief fupport is fuppofed to be from a flower that grows plentifully in the neighbourhood, fomewhat refembling a tulip; from this flower iffues a juice equal in fweetnefs and thicknefs to fyrup; and, when boiled, it is good for complaints in the breaft, and alfo for young children.

The remainder of the road from Muffleburg to Cape Town is, in general, very pleafant; numerous villas being interfperfed on both fides of the road. In particular, as you round Table Hill, towards Cape Town, the rifing appearance of Conftantia, where

D 4   the

the famous wine is made, has a won-
derful effect upon the traveller; the
fituation of it being under the Ta-
ble-Mountain, about three miles from
Muffelburg, and ten from Cape Town.

At fix o'clock in the evening we
reached the end of our journey; moft
completely joftled and tired. We
were all lodged at Mrs. de Witt's,
mother to the abovementioned gentleman, well known by the Englifh
frequenting the Cape: her bulk,
comparatively fpeaking, was nearly
equal to that of a Dutch man of war,
and, being remarkably low in ftature,
her fize was rendered ftill more confpicuous. She received us with much
complacency, and immediately procured a little cargo of bread and but-

2   ter,

ter, which I believe we all relished
very much, having had no overplus
in that article during our paffage. The
countenance of the good lady was
pleafing, her manner engaging, and
her motherly attention, during our
fhort *fejour* at her habitation, fuch
as I fhall ever remember with the
greateft degree of fatisfaction. Mifs
J. de Witt did not make her appearance that evening; the eldeft daughter was not very converfible; and a
young lady, a relation, was remarkably bafhful. Thus fituated, we were
obliged to amufe ourfelves with our
own private remarks, until fupper
was ready; a meal which, in this
town, is diftinguifhed for fubftantial
difhes; and, what is always moft
welcome to voyagers, plenty of vegetables,

tables, which are as fweet as they can poffibly be; for the fituation of this climate is fo happy, that all European and moft tropical fruits and vegetables grow as well as in their native foils.

On the 24th of June, after a good night's repofe, I arofe particularly thankful to Providence for His protection ; and offered up my daily fupplication for the health of the affectionate ties I had left in England. Curiofity then directed my fteps to a window, whence I beheld the fmall remains of his Majefty's fhip the Guardian, commanded by Lieutenant Riou, an officer confpicuous for prefence of mind in the moft imminent danger, and for feelingly recommending

ding his mother and fisters to the notice of his honourable employers. By
dint of the greatest exertion he brought
his ship to the Cape, and saved the
lives of those of the crew who remained with him : as a reward for
his services, he has since been made
a post-captain.   To avoid as much as
possible any disagreeable reflections
which might arise from the idea of a
probability of our sharing the fate of
the above vessel (as the Gorgon was
the first ship commissioned for the relief of the colony, after the fatal loss
of the Guardian), I hastened to my
companions, and was, for the first
time, surprized with a Cape breakfast, which certainly merits many
encomiums : it is customary to ar-
range out the table as for dinner,
except

except its being covered with all forts
of fruit; againſt each perſon is placed
a knife, a plate, and a napkin; thus
feated, the lady of the houſe makes
tea and coffee at a ſide-table, which
the ſlaves hand round to the company.

The day being very rainy, and
our baggage advancing ſlower than
we had done, it was mutually agreed
to remain at home. We were viſited
by Mynheer Van Graaffe, the Governor, who was at that time about to
reſign; alſo by Colonel Burrington
and other Gentlemen.

A deſcription of Cape Town having
repeatedly been given by authors of
knowledge and taſte; I only intend,
with

with fubmiffion to my readers, to commit to paper my own flender remarks on the various objects which engaged my attention.

The town I thought both clean and pleafant; its environs afford feveral delightful rides : the road to the Company's houfe, by the fea-fide, brought to my recollection one from Puerta Colonela, at Leghorn, round the Lazarettos, to Monti Negro. I was ftruck with the uncommon dexterity of the Cape-drivers, who manage eight horfes in hand, and turn the corners with the greateft fwiftnefs. The carriages ufed for thefe excurfions are entirely open, and confift, fome of two, and others of four feats.

In

In this town there are no public
amufements, nor any particular pro-
menades, excepting the Governor's
garden, at the end of which there is
a very large aviary. There are not
any public fhops, as in other towns:
the merchants difpofe of their goods,
both by wholefale and retail, in the
following method : if you wifh to
make any purchafe you fend for a
large book, upon the leaves of which
are pafted patterns of edgings, di-
mities, filks, muflins, &c. with the
prices annexed ; and if you make any
large purchafe, you go and view the
different articles in the parlours.
Butcher, baker, &c. are all equally
private; in fact, the moft pleafing
fight is in the market-place at day-
break,

break, when the flaves, moftly two
by two, bring their bafkets by the
means of poles on their fhoulders.
Oftrich feathers are very plentiful.
There is alfo every fort of fruit in
great abundance ; that which was
moft remarkable to me was the rofe-
apple, not having met with it in
any of my former travels in France,
Spain, and Italy : there is a faintnefs
in the tafte of this apple which few
palates would approve of ; but the
odoriferous fmell it difperfes around
renders it very acceptable when placed
amongft other fruit.

The women of the Cape are remarkable for their bulk ; which I am
apt to attribute to their going without
ftays, and fitting much in the houfe

with

with their feet continually lifted on a
chair. They have good teeth, and
in general their features are pleafing;
after marriage they are totally neglect-
ful of their perfons.

Neither hat nor bonnet is fafhion-
able amongft them; high caps, with
cloaks or fhawls, are worn in their
ftead; the latter they have frequent
opportunities of receiving, in return
for the hofpitality fhewn to our Bri-
tifh Eaft India fhips.

The churches at Cape Town are
open at eight in the morning, when
the genteel claffes go in fedan chairs,
which are ufually kept in the entrance
of their houfes.

CHAP.

C H A P. IV.

Vifit Colonel Gordon.—Arrival of the
Neptune.—Receive intelligence from
New South Wales.—Arrival of Cap-
tain Patterfon and his Lady.—A
Cape Dance.—A Hottentot Song.—
Vifit Mr. Vandrian's Brewery.—Pre-
pare for our Departure.—Set fail.

OUR baggage arrived the next
day, and we were bufily employed, having engaged ourfelves to dine
with Colonel Gordon. The hour of
dinner was two o'clock ; the Colonel obligingly fent his carriage for us,
which was very acceptable, the wea-

ther

ther being intenfely hot, and the
pavement intolerably bad. The Villa
where the Colonel refides is fituated
a few miles from the town, on the
fummit of a hill commanding a moft
pleafant and extenfive view by fea and
land. The good Colonel is already
well known for his Mufeum, and
Manufcripts relative to Natural Hif-
tory, and his many enterprifing jour-
neys to the interior parts of that
country; for which he was eminent-
ly qualified on account of his extenfive knowledge of the language,
manners, and cuftoms of the Hotten-
tots, by whom he is almoft adored.——
The refpect and regard which I bear to
this family forbids my paffing over in
filence the polite and friendly attention I received from Mrs. Gordon, who

is

is a Swifs lady, and who moſt agreeably acquiefces in whatever may tend
to render thofe comfortable who have
the happinefs of being ranked amongſt
her acquaintance. After what I have
faid, it will eafily be fuppofed that
their children are taught the fame
engaging attention to ſtrangers.

On the next day, the Neptune and
the Lady Juliana anchored in Falfe
Bay ; both of them had been ſhips
fent out by Government with Convicts and Stores to the colony of New
South Wales, and, after having ful-
filled their contract with Government,
were permitted to go to China, to take
in a freight of Teas on account of the
Eaſt-India Company. We did not
receive any favourable account of the

E 2　　　　　　place

place we were fhortly going to vifit;
on the contrary, we learnt from the
commander of the Neptune, Mr. D.
Trail, that, on his leaving it, there
were only fix months provifions in
the Settlement, at full allowance;
we alfo learnt the difappointment of
the Governor and Officers of that Colony at the non-arrival of the Guardian:—in fhort, every circumftance
ferved to affure us how anxioufly they
waited the appearance of our happy
bark; and made Captain Parker as
anxious to relieve them.

About this time the arrival of the
Britannia and Albemarle tranfports
was announced: this circumftance
afforded us confiderable fatisfaction, as
we were in expectation of again meeting

ing with Mrs. Patterſon, the Lady of Captain Patterſon of the new corps. This gentleman once accompanied Colonel Gordon in his excurſion up the country. An unexpected meeting with thoſe of our kingdom is always agreeable to travellers : it proved ſo to us ; and the more eſpecially as it chiefly conſiſted of thoſe who were engaged upon ſervices, ſimilar in their nature with our intended voyage.

But, though ſurrounded with novelties and amuſements, I could not forget the perilous ſituation of my huſband, who was gone to bring the ſhip round to Table Bay, the winter-ſeaſon rendering it very unſafe on account of the Monſoons which are pre-

E 3   valent

valent at that time of the year; but, thanks to the Supreme Being! the ſhip appeared in ſight on Sunday the 17th of July, and Captain Parker came on ſhore to dinner. We received another invitation from Mrs. Gordon, and accordingly went in the afternoon to Green Point to tea; after which, we returned home to ſupper, and the evening concluded with dancing, which they are remarkably fond of at this town; particularly a dance ſomewhat like the *Allemande*, excepting the figure, which is not variable, and the long continuance of turning round: it is ſurprizing that the ladies are not giddy with the ſwiftneſs of the motion; for it would certainly turn any perſon's head unaccuſtomed to it.

The

The next morning we again vifited
the hofpitable villa, where we were
regaled in a manner that befpoke the
attention of the providers: during a
defert that would have gained ap-
plaufe from the niceft Epicure, fing-
ing was introduced, in the courfe of
which we were favoured with a *Hottentot* fong from the Colonel: to defcribe any part of it would be impoffible; but, without a wifh to of-
fend, I muft fay that it appeared to
me the very reverfe of all that
is mufical or harmonious; and the
Colonel, who gave us ftrict charge
not to be frightened with what we
were to hear, feemed to enjoy the
laughter it occafioned. Different
fongs having gone round, the Colonel's fon amufed us with feveral pieces

E 4   upon

upon the organ ; and fhortly after we were agreeably furprized with the bands belonging to the regiments without : nor did this conclude the amufement ; for, after drinking coffee, we danced until our return into town, when the fame mufic accompanied us, to prevent, I fuppofe, our fpirits from drooping at the thought of leaving fuch good company.

The next day Captain Patterfon and his Lady arrived from Falfe Bay ; who, fortunately for our little parties, remained at the houfe in which we refided. Through the friendly introduction of this gentleman I became one of the party at Mr. Vandrian's ; and I cannot but acknowledge the polite attention I received from this family

family during my ſhort acquaintance.

On the 24th, a ſelect party of us
dined at Colonel Gordon's, where we
met Colonel Burrington *, Major De
Liſle, with ſome other Dutchmen, and
Mr. Pitt, a relation of Lord Chatham,
who was fortunately ſaved out of the
wreck of the Guardian. We were occupied in feaſting and ſinging till the
evening, when we returned home,
and found the company waiting for us.
Upon our arrival, the dances immediately began ; and, after eating an
excellent ſupper, we retired to our

* Whilſt writing the above, intelligence has
been received of the death of this gentleman, in
an engagement with the Rohilla Chiefs, on the
26th of October, 1794.

apart-

apartments ; but, from the cool..efs of the night, the moon fhining delightfully, and the mufic parading the ftreets, we were unwilling to confign ourfelves to " dull oblivion."

The next day we vifited Mr. Vandrian, at the Brewery ; where we met with a welcome reception : the houfe and gardens are very pleafant; the brewery is an extenfive building, fituated between Cape Town and Falfe Bay, very near the latter; and, ftrange to fay, not far diftant from Paradife ! a fpot of ground fo called, from the fituation ; and about which the Silver Tree grows in great perfection : neither is it far from Conftantia.

The Governor, having rode out that morning, ftopped and joined the

party,

party, who were then at dinner ; and, the evening proving rainy, we returned with him in his *voiture d'Hollande*.

The following day we were bufily employed in getting our cloaths ready for fea, and in fending them on-board, as we expected to embark that afternoon ; however, the bufinefs of the fhip not being actually accomplifhed, we flept on fhore that night ; and on the enfuing morning, the 31ft of July, we all repaired on-board, efcorted to the key by the greater part of Mr. de Witt's family : Mr. Peter de Witt accompanied us on-board, and faw us under weigh.

CHAP.

CHAP. V.

The voyage continued—a melancholy accident ; singular instance of fraternal affection—death of Lieutenant Ross—a dreadful storm—the falling of a ball of fire—observations and reflections.

DURING our residence at the Cape, great care had been taken amply to provide for the remainder of our voyage ; the crew were well supplied with fresh provisions, and we returned to our little sea-amusements in peace and tranquillity of mind.

With

With my companion Mrs. King, and the fociety of the fhip, I feldom, if ever, found any thing unpleafant, except the pitching of the fhip, which motion proved very difagreeable to me to the end of our voyage.

We proceeded favourably on our paffage, having, in general, good weather, and brifk winds, until the 7th of September, when we met with the following melancholy occurrences. At 6 o'clock, P. M. a carpenter fell overboard; the cutter was immediately fent to refcue him, if poffible, from the mercilefs waves; but to no effect, the fea running high, and the wind blowing frefh : one difmal hour had fcarcely elapfed when the cutter returned,

returned, and, while hoifting it in, another poor man fell overboard : the cutter was again fent out ; but, alas ! the earneft attempts of the failors to fave the life of their comrade unfortunately proved abortive ; his brother, who was in the boat, had been refcued by the deceafed from a fimilar accident only a few months before; his gratitude to, and affection for, this brother, loft before him, drove him into a delirium ; in which dreadful ftate he continued for fome time. A difmal fky and a deluge of rain concluded this difaftrous and eventful night. The enfuing morning was equally ftormy as the preceding evening, and the weather continued much the fame until the 11th, when we faw the Coaft of New Holland.

In

In the evening of this day we had the misfortune of lofing Mr. George Rofs, midfhipman, after a fevere ill-nefs fince leaving the Cape. This young gentleman was the fon of Lieutenant Rofs of the Navy, and brought up at Portfmouth Academy; he was a very promifing youth, and his death was fincerely regretted by all his fhip-mates, and the fuperior officers of the fhip, for his attention to his duty. The fame melancholy evening died fuddenly James Key, a feaman. The enfuing day the bodies of the deceafed were committed to the deep, after having performed the ufual funeral fervice.

On the 12th we had frefh gales, with favourable weather, which continued

continued until the 17th, when we came in fight of Mount Dromedary, fo called from the fimilarity of its fhape. This day we were engaged to dine with the officers in the ward-room : under the expectation of arriving fhortly at Port Jackfon, the time paffed away very fociably ; but a fudden fquall and perverfe winds coming on, deprived us of the fatis-faction of reaching the wifhed-for haven for three long days—at leaft they appeared fo to every one of us ; when we reflected that the colony ftood in fuch great need of the fup-plies with which we were fo plen-teoufly ftored : however, with pa-tience, the fovereign remedy of all evils, and the travellers beft fupport, I paffed the time in adjufting the ca-bin,

bin, and in other preparations prior
to our going on ſhore.

The enſuing day, being Sunday,
was pleaſant and ſerene, as if to afford us an opportunity of imploring
a continuance of the Divine Protection, which we had hitherto experienced in a ſingular degree.

On Monday the 19th, at noon, we
were in latitude 35°. 15″. S. and
longitude 149°. 26″. E. from the
meridian of Greenwich, when a point
of land appeared in ſight, called by
Captain Cook *Long Noſe*, on account of
its pointed ſhape. At ſun-ſet the hovering clouds ſeemed to forebode the event
of the evening ; at eight came on a
tremendous thunder ſquall, attended

F   with

with moft dreadful lightning and conftant heavy rains, which continued upwards of an hour and a half. About *half* paft *eight* the lightning ftruck the pole of the main-top-gallant-maft, fhivered it and the head of the maft entirely to pieces ; thence it communicated to the main-top-maft, under the hounds, and fplit it exactly in the middle, above *one third* down the maft ; it next took the main-maft by the main-yard, on the larboard fide, and in a fpherical direction ftruck it in fix different places; the fhock electrified every perfon on the quarter-deck; thofe who were unfortunately near the main-maft were knocked down, but recovered in a few minutes : this continued until about *half* paft *ten*, when a moft

awful

awful fpectacle prefented itfelf to the
view of thofe on deck; whilft we
who were below felt a fudden fhock,
which gave us every reafon to fear
that the fhip had ftruck againft a
rock; from which dreadful apprehenfion we were however relieved
upon being informed that it was occafioned by a ball of fire which fell at
that moment. The lightning alfo
broke over the fhip in every direction:
it was allowed to be a difmal refem-
blance of a befieged garrifon; and,
if I might hazard an opinion, I fhould
think it was the effect of an earth-
quake. The fea ran high, and feemed to foam with anger at the feeble
refiftance which our lone bark occafioned. At midnight the wind fhifted to the weftward, which brought

on

oh fine clear weather, and I found myſelf once more at leiſure to anticipate the ſatisfaction which our arrival would diffuſe throughout the colony ; for, owing to the loſs of his majeſty's ſhip The Guardian, the governor and officers were reduced to ſuch ſcanty allowance, that, in addition to the fatigues and hardſhips which they had experienced when the colony was in its infant ſtate, they were obliged, from a ſcarcity of proviſions, to toil through the weariſome day with the anxious and melancholy expectations of increaſing difficulties. What then could afford us more heart-felt pleaſure than the near event of relieving them ? for it is ſurely happineſs to ſuccour the diſtreſſed ; a ſatisfaction we fully experienced.

perienced. Our defire of reaching the colony was alfo increafed by the reflection, that the greater part of the marine officers were to return with us once more to vifit Old England, and to render happy fuch of their friends and relations as had lingered out their abfence with many an aching heart. With what anxiety did they await the fhip's arrival! with what eagernefs did they haften on-board! The circumftances are too deeply engraven on my memory ever to be eradicated; but, alas! my pen is utterly incompetent to the tafk of defcribing our feelings on this occafion.

CHAP.

CHAP. VI.

*Arrive at Port Jackſon—Governor
King and Captain Parker wait upon
Governor Phillip with the diſpatches—Account of ſhips arrived ···
the harbour ; and of a dreadful
mortality which had taken place on-
board the tranſports—Intereſting
particulars reſpecting the propriety
of eſtabliſhing a whale-fiſhery on the
coaſt of New Holland.*

AT ſun-riſe we ſaw the coaſt of
New Holland, extending from Souṭh
Weſt to North Weſt, diſtant from the
neareſt part about nine or ten miles.
During the night we were driven to
the

the Northward, and paffed Port Jackfon, the port to which we were bound;
however, on the enfuing day, the
21ft, we arrived fafe in the above
harbour. As foon as the fhip anchored feveral officers came on-board;
and, fhortly after, Governor King, accompanied by Captain Parker, went
on fhore, and waited on his Excellency Governor Phillip, with the
government-difpatches : they were
welcome vifitors ; and I may fafely
fay, that the arrival of our fhip dif-
fufed univerfal joy throughout the
whole fettlement.

We found lying here his Majefty's
armed tender The Supply, with her
lower mafts both out of repair ; they
were fo bad, that fhe was obliged to

have

have others made of the wood of the country, which was procured with great difficulty, feveral hundred trees being cut down without finding any fufficiently found at the core. Lieutenant Bowen, with four fail of tranfports under his direction, was arrived here; alfo The Mary-Anne, a tranfport-fhip, that had been fent out alone, with only women-convicts and provifions on-board.

A dreadful mortality had taken place on-board of moft of the tranfports which had been fent to this country; the poor miferable objects that were landed died in great numbers, fo that they were foon reduced to at leaft *one third* of the number that quitted England.

" Their

" Their appearance," to ufe the words of Captain Parker, " will be " ever frefh in my memory. I vifited " the hofpital, and was furrounded " by mere fkeletons of men—in every " bed, and on every fide, lay the " dying and the dead. Horrid fpec- " tacle! it makes me fhudder when " I reflect, that it will not be the laft " exhibition of this kind of human " mifery that will take place in this " country, whilft the prefent method " of tranfporting thefe miferable " wretches is purfued; for, the more " of them that die, the more it re- " dounds to the intereft of the fhip " owners and mafters, who are paid " fo much a-head by government, for " each individual, whether they ar- " rive in the colony or not."

But

But to return to my narrative.—On
the 25th, in confequence of the an-
niverfary of his majefty's acceffion to
the throne, his Excellency Governor
Phillip gave a public dinner to all
the army and navy officers in the colony. The Gorgon dreffed fhip as
well as her fcanty allowance of colours
would permit; and, at the ufual hour,
fired twenty-one guns.

About this time, Mr. Melvin, maf-
ter of The Britannia tranfport, arrived here; with this, and with feveral other gentlemen, Captain Parker
held various conferences on the propriety of eftablifhing a Whale-Fifhery on the Coaft of New Holland.
Minutes of thefe conferences were
preferved

preferved by my hufband; and, as they appear to me rather interefting, I fhall take the liberty of inferting them in this place.

" Mr. Melvin gave it as his opinion that a very good Whale-Fifhery might be eftablifhed upon this coaft; and that fifh were infinitely more nume-rous than on the American. In his paffage from Van Deiman's Land to Port Jackfon, he afferted that he faw more fhoals of fpermaceti whales in the courfe of that voyage, than in any one of a great number which he had made in the South Whale-Fifhery. This afternoon he failed, upon ex-periment, accompanied by the Wil-liam and Anne, Edward Bunker, maf-ter. The day after their leaving Port Jackfon,

Jackfon, they fell-in with a fhoal of whales; the boats belonging to the two fhips ftruck feven of them; but the wind blew fo hard that each fhip faved but one; and, in confequence of the weather, were obliged to return from the cruize.

As foon as the agreement between Government and the fhips had ended, which was when they had landed their convicts and difcharged their lading, the mafters of them were at full liberty to proceed upon their owners' employ Five of the number had permiffion from the Eaft India Company to load with cotton at Bombay; the others, being fifhery-fhips, went out and returned frequently. During the time of our ftay at Port Jackfon,

Jackfon, they faw abundance of fifh; but, always meeting with tempeftuous weather and a ftrong current fetting to windward, their fuccefs was not adequate to their expectations. One of them, named the Matilda, took three fifh, which yielded about thirty barrels of oil, and the mafter told me that it was in its quality more valuable, by *ten* pounds in the 'ton, than the oil which they procured on the coaft of America. One of them gave me a fmall keg of it, which I brought home with me as a fpecimen. They alfo told me, that nothing but the fear of lofing the time of their employers prevented them from continuing on this coaft, for they had many good harbours to run into if need required; an advantage of confiderable importance,

tance, as it enabled them always to have a good supply of water, which was not the case when fishing on the American coast: they had also great relief from wild herbs gathered here, particularly that called Sweet Tea, which makes a very pleasant and wholesome beverage. These, with other considerations, were sufficient to influence those employed in the Whale-Fishery to prefer this coast to the other, where they have no port to go into, as, by treaty, they are not to approach nearer than one hundred leagues of the shore: in consequence of which, their crew must be greatly infected with the scurvy, for want of that assistance which they can so plenteously meet with on the coast of New South Wales. They

have

have alfo an opportunity of keeping their fhips in much better repair, having harbours to go into when neceffity required, whereas on the coaft of America it is quite the re-verfe.

New Holland abounds in good har-bours; we have thoroughly invefti-gated the greater part of them, and there are many others at prefent but imperfectly known ; yet, if a Whale-Fifhery were once eftablifhed, they would foon become familiar to us ; and, if peculiar emoluments were granted to Ships that took fifh on this coaft in preference to that of America, great advantages might accrue to Go-vernment therefrom : the number of veffels which would be in that em-

ploy

ploy muft greatly leffen the freight of tranfports, and give us continual opportunities of fupplying the fettlement at a moderate expence to government: it would alfo be an encouragement to fettlers to go over ; and until that takes place the maintaining the Colony of New South Wales will be a continually accumulating burthen to the mother-country. Were we to fend fettlers from England, with fome little property of their own, and to give the men fufficient encouragement by allotting them ground, building them convenient houfes, allowing them a certain number of convicts, giving them tools of hufbandry, feeds of various kinds adequate to the number of acres in their poffeffion, and victualling them and their men, for

at

at leaft eighteen months, out of the public ftores, at the expiration of which time they and their men were to provide for themfelves——Were we to do thefe things, it might probably be able to fupport itfelf in a few years.

But to return to the Whale Fifhery: it might be carried on by fmall veffels at the different harbours with which we are at prefent acquainted ; if they contained cafks enough to hold the blubber which two or three Whales might produce, and were able to carry three or four Whale-Boats, they would be fufficiently large. When they took any fifh, if it were not convenient to run for Port Jackfon, let them make any of the other harbours, immediately boil down the oil, and then

watch

watch for the opportunity to proceed to fea again. It is to be obferved, that, at the full and change of the Moon, the weather is very tempeftuous and unfettled on this coaft, and alfo that there is a ftrong current always fetting to windward; the harder it blows, the ftronger it fets, and caufes a turbulent, irregular, and very high fea. In the courfe of a feafon thefe fmall veffels would in all probability procure a fufficient quantity of oil to load fuch fhips as fhould be fent from England to receive it; but, if any objection be made to fmall craft from the apprehenfion of convicts running away with them, let all the fhips that Government take up belong to the Whale-fifhery; let them fail from England in the Months of October, November,

November, and December; and after
having landed their ſtores, or whatever they may have brought out for
Government, let them refit their ſhips
and then proceed on the fiſhery, returning to Port Jackſon when they
want refreſhments, or into any of the
harbours with which we are acquainted Lieutenant Bowen, of the At-
lantic tranſport, diſcovered a bay,
which, in honour to Sir John Jervis,
he named after him. This bay has
been ſince explored by Mr. Weather-
head, maſter of The Mary and Anne
tranſport; who, in one of his cruizes
after whales, was twice there, and
has given me a draught of it.

There are two other ports known
to the Northward of Port Jackſon;

the

the firft is *Broken Bay*, which has been well furveyed by Captain Hunter, of his majefty's fhip The Sirius ; and is a very fine harbour, forming into different branches : one branch enters the river Hawkesbury ; another runs to the Weftward, and forms a fine piece of water, which has been named, by Governor Phillip, *Pitt-water*. The next harbour to the Northward of this is Port Stephens, which has not been explored ; but fome of the fifh-fhips have been clofe in with it, and make no doubt but that it is a very good port."

CHAP.

CHAP. VII.

*Governor Phillip breakfasts on-board—
visit Sidney Cove—go on-shore—short
description of shrubs, birds, beasts,
&c of Botany Bav—excursion to,
and description of, Paramatta—visit
the Governor.*

BUT to return to my narrative.—
On the 3ᵒth Governor Phillip did us
the honour to breakfast on-board; so
did also Mr. Collins, Judge A vocate;
and Mr Palmer, the Commiffary.
The converfation was very interefting;
the one party anxioufly making en-
quiries after their relatives in Eng

land; and the other attentively lif
tening to the troubles and anxieties
which had attended the improve-
ments made in that diftant colony.
When the company returned on-
fhore, we amufed ourfelves with the
pleafing novelties of *Sidney Cove*, fo
named by the Governor in honour of
Lord Sidney: from this Cove, although it is very rocky, a moft pleafant verdure proceeds on each fide:
the little habitations on fhore, together with the canoes around us,
and the uncommon manners of the
natives in them were more than fufficient amufements for that day; the
next was occupied in receiving vifits
from feveral officers belonging to
this fettlement.

When

When we went on fhore, we were
all admiration at the natural beauties
raifed by the hand of Providence
without expence or toil : I mean the
various flowery fhrubs, natives of this
country, that grow apparently from
rock itfelf. The gentle afcents, the
winding valleys, and the abundance
of flowering fhrubs, render the face
of the country very delightful. The
fhrub which moft attracted my attention was one which bears a white
flower, very much refembling our
Englifh Hawthorn ; the fmell of it is
both fweet and fragrant, and per-
fumes the air around to a confiderable
diftance. Theie is alfo plenty of
grafs, which grows with the greateft
vigour and luxuriance, but which,

how-

however, as Captain Tench juftly
obferves, is not of the fineft quality,
and is found to agree better with
horfes and cows than with fheep.

In Botany Bay there are not many
land fowls : of the larger fort, only
eagles were feen ; of the fmaller
kind, though not numerous, 'there is
a variety, from the fize of a wren to
that of a lark ; all of which are remarkable for fine loud notes, and
beautiful plumage, particularly thofe
of the paroquet kind. Crows are alfo
found here, exactly the fame as thofe
in England. But defcriptions, infinitely beyond the abilities of her
who now, folely for the benefit of
her little flock, is advifed to fet forth
this narrative, having been already
pub-

publifhed, it would be prefumptive to attempt any thing farther.

Our amufements here, although neither numerous nor expenfive, were to me perfectly novel and agreeable: the fatherly attention of the good Governor upon all occafions, with the friendly politenefs of the officers rendered our *féjour* perfectly happy and comfortable.

After our arrival here, Governor King and his Lady, refided on fhore at Governor Phillip's, to whofe houfe I generally repaired after breakfafting on-board: indeed it always proved a home for me; under this hofpitable roof, I have often ate part of a Kingaroo, with as much glee as if I had

been

been a partaker of fome of the greateft delicacies of this metropolis, although latterly I was cloyed with them, and found them very difagreeable. The prefents of eggs, milk, and vegetables, which I was often favoured with from the officers on fhore, were always very acceptable ; and the precaution which Captain Parker had taken, previous to our departure from the Cape of Good Hope, made me fully contented with my fituation.

Our parties generally confifted of Mrs. King, Mr. Johnfon, and the Ladies who refided at the colony. We made feveral pleafant excurfions up the Cove to the fettlement called *Paramatta*. The numerous branches, creeks, and inlets, that are formed in

3   the

the harbour of Port Jackfon, and the
wood that covers all their fhores down
to the very edge of the water, make
the fcenery beautiful : the North
branch is particularly fo, from the
floping of its fhores, the interfperfion
of tufted woods, verdant lawns, and
the fmall Iflands, which are covered
with trees, fcattered up and down.

Upon our firft arrival at *Paramatta*,
I was furprifed to find that fo great a
progrefs had been made in this new
fettlement, which contains above one
thoufand convicts, befides the military. There is a very good level road,
of great breadth, that runs nearly a
mile in a ftraight direction from the
landing place to the Governor's houfe,
which is a fmall convenient building,
placed

placed upon a gentle afcent, and furrounded by about a couple of acres of
garden ground: this fpot is called
Rofe-Hill. On both fides of the road
are fmall thatched huts, at an equal
diftance from each other. After
fpending the day very agreeably at
the Governor's, we repaired to the
lodging which had been provided for
us, where we had the comfort of a
large wood fire, and found every thing
perfectly quiet, although furrounded
by more than one thoufand convicts.
We enjoyed our night's repofe; and
in the morning without the previous
aid of toilet or mirror, we fet out for
the Governor's to breakfaft, and returned with the fame party on the
enfuing day.

This

This little excurfion afforded us an opportunity of noticing the beautiful plumage of the birds in general, and of the *Emu* in particular, two of which we difcovered in the woods : their plumage is remarkably fine, and rendered particularly curious, as each neu has two feathers generally of a light brown; the wings are fo fmall as hardly to deferve the name; and, though incapable of flying, they can run with fuch fwiftnefs that a greyhound can with difficulty keep pace with them. The flefh taftes fomewhat like beef.

In this cove there are fome cool receffes, where with Captain Parker and the officers I have been many times

times revived after the intenſe heat of the day, taking with us what was neceſſary to quench our thirſt.

Here we have feaſted upon Oiſters juſt taken out of the ſea;—the attention of our ſailors, and their care in opening and placing them round their hats, in lieu of plates, by no means diminiſhing the ſatisfaction we had in eating them. Indeed, the Oiſters here are both good and plentiful: I have purchaſed a large *three-quart* bowl of them, for a pound and a half of tobacco, beſides having them opened for me into the bargain.

CHAP.

CHAP. VIII.

*Defcription of the inhabitants of New
South Wales—their huts—their ex-
traordinary honefty — account of
Banalong—an inftance of his fenfi-
bility.—obfervations on the Slave
Trade.*

THE Inhabitants of New South
Wales, both male and female, go without apparel. Their colour is of a
dingy copper; their nofe is broad and
flat, their lips wide and thick, and
their eyes circular. From a difagreeable practice they have of rubbing
themfelves with fifh-oil, they fmell fo
loath-

loathfome, that it is almoft impoffible
to approach them without difguft.

The men in general appeared to
be from five feet fix to five feet nine
inches high, are rather flender, but
ftraight and well made : they have
bufhy beards, and the hair on their
heads is ftuck full with the teeth of
fifh, and bits of fhells : they alfo or-
nament themfelves with a fifh-bone
faftened in the griftle of the nofe,
which makes them appear really
frightful; and are generally armed
with a ftick about a yard long, and a
lance which they throw with confiderable velocity.

The ftature of the women is fomewhat lefs than that of the men—their
nofes

nofes are broad, their mouths wide, and their lips thick. They are extremely negligent of their perfons, and are filthy to a degree fcarcely credible : their faces and bodies are befmeared with the fat of animals, and the falutary cuftom of wafhing feems entirely unknown to them.

Their huts or habitations are conftructed in the moft rude and barbarous manner : they confift of pieces of bark laid together fomewhat in the form of an oven, with a fmall entrance at one end. Their fole refidence, however, is not in thefe huts ; on the contrary, they depend lefs on them for fhelter than on the numerous excavations which are formed in the rocks by the wafhing

H   of

of the fea; and it is no uncommon thing to fee fifty or fixty of them comfortably lodged in one of thefe caves.

Notwithftanding the general appearance of the natives, I never felt the leaft fear when in their company, being always with a party more than fufficient for my protection. I have been feated in the woods with twelve or fourteen of them, men, women, and children. Had I objected, or fhewn any difguft at their appearance, it would have given them fome reafon to fuppofe that I was not what they term their *damely*, or friend; and would have rendered my being in their company not only unpleafant, but unfafe.

Before

Before I conclude my defcription
cf the natives, it is but juftice to remark, that, in comparifon with the
inhabitants of moft of the South-Sea
Iflands, they appear very little given
to thieving; and their confidence in
the honefty of one another is fo great,
that they will leave their fpears and
other implements on the fea-fhore,
in full and perfect fecurity of their
remaining untouched.

From the treatment which I in-
variably experienced, I am inclined to
think favourably of them; and fully
believe that they would never injure
our people, were they not firft of-
fended by them.

I can

I cannot help obferving that one of
the men had a moft engaging deportment; his countenance was pleafing,
and his manners far beyond what I
could poffibly have expected. He
was pleafed to feat himfelf by me,
changed names with Captain Parker,
and took particular notice of the
travelling knife and fork with which
I was eating, and which I did myfelf
the fatisfaction to give him : he paid
us a vifit on-board the enfuing day,
and fhewed me that he had not loft
my prefent, but made ufe of it,
though fomewhat aukwardly, whilft
he demolifhed *two* or *three* pounds of
the fhip's pork.

The

The natives very frequently furrounded our veffel with their canoes.
The women often held up their little
ones, as if anxious to have them noticed by us. Sometimes, for the fake
of amufement, I have thrown them
ribbands and other trifles, which
they would as frequently tye round
their toes as any other part of their
perfon.

Since my return to England, Banalong, one of the natives brought
hither by Governor Phillip, came to
fee me. To defcribe the pleafure that
overfpread this poor fellow's countenance when my little girl prefented to
him the picture of her dear father,
is impoffible; it was then that the

H 3   tear

tear of fenfibility trickled down his cheeks; he immediately recognized thofe features which will never be obliterated from my memory, and fpoke, with all the energy of Nature, of the pleafing excurfion which they had made together up the country. The above is one amongft many inftances which I could relate of the natural goodnefs of their hearts; and I flatter myfelf that the time is haftening when they will no longer be confidered as mere favages;—and wherefore fhould they?

" Fleecy locks, and black complexion,
  " Cannot forfeit Nature's claim:
" Skins may differ, but affection
  " Dwells in white and black the fame."

CHAP.

CHAP. IX.

Preparations for our departure—repair on-board—set sail—discover Lord Howe's Island—Mount Lidgbird—Mount Gower—Three Kings Head Island—New Zealand—Cape Maria.

IN the course of this month (October), the Britannia transport anchored at this place, as did also the Admiral Barrington. The arrival of the latter afforded us the pleasure of seeing Mrs. Patterson again, whose company added much to the happiness of our little parties. The 25th was quite a busy day with us, it being the commemoration of His Majesty's accession to the throne: after amusing our-

selves

felves in the morning with looking
at fome fhips which were bufily employed in going out of the cove on a
fifhing expedition, and the *full dreſs*
of our bark in compliment to the
day, we repaired to the Governor's,
whofe unremitting attention to his
guefts rendered the day very agreeable, could we but have forgotten
that it was the eve of our feparation
from Captain King and his Lady,
whofe affability had fo much contri-
buted to the pleafantry of our voyage
thus far; and who, with Captain
and Mrs. Patterfon and feveral other
military officers deftined for Norfolk
Ifland, fet fail the next day, accompanied to the end of the cove by the
Governor, Judge Advocate, Captain
Parker, and many others, who were

anxious

anxious to be in their company as long as poffible,

From the firft of our arrival at Port Jackfon, no time had been loft in preparing for our return to England. The embarkation of the marines, with their wives twenty five in number, and their children forty-feven, the caulking of the veffel, the clergyman of the New Corps coming onboard to read divine fervice for the laft time, in fhort every thing began to remind me of our departure.

The fhip, when ready for fea, was very differently ftored to what it was when we left the Cape of Good Hope in July. In lieu of live ftock and all kind of neceffary provifions, our

bark

bark was now crowded with Kanga-
roos, Oppofums, and every curiofity
which that country produced. The
quarter-deck was occupied with fhrubs
and plants, whilft the cabin was hung
around with fkins of animals. We
had alfo procured a variety of birds.
I was fo fortunate as to bring to England a bronzed wing, and two pair
of Norfolk Ifland pigeons ; they are
now alive and well, and are, I believe
the only birds of the kind ever
brought to this country.

The uniform attention which the
Governor paid us during our fhort
ftay at the colony will always be
remembered with fingular fatisfaction :—he may be juftly called, like
the Monarch of Great Britain, " *The*
" *Father*

" *Father of his People*;" and the Convict, who has forfaken the crimes
that fent him to this country, looks
up to him with reverence, and enjoys
the reward of his induftry in peace
and thankfulnefs:—indeed, the kind-
nefs which we experienced from all
around was fuch, that to have left the
colony without a confiderable degree
of regret at parting from them would
have fhewn much ingratitude.

On the 17th of December, after
fupping at the Governor's, we repaired
on-board, where every one was bufily
engaged in lafhing and fecuring fuch
things as were intended to be convey-
ed to England : it was my occupation
to look after the birds, and to place
them in the fafeft and moft convenient
manner I poffibly could.

18th. Anchor

18th. Anchor being weighed, we set fail at 7 o'clock P. M.

19th. Freſh breezes, and rather ſqually.

20th. We found ourſelves at the North Head of Port Jackſon, with freſh breezes. At midnight hard ſqualls from all parts of the compaſs.

21ſt. At 4 A. M. heavy rain with lightning; at 6, violent ſqualls of wind, with a deluge of rain, ſevere thunder and lightning, the wind fly-ing around the compaſs, and the ſhip labouring very much. At 10, we brought-to, the unſettled weather not permitting us to ſail, except on
the

the Southerly tack. At 8 P. M. the
fea ftruck the veffel on the ftarboard
quarter, which occafioned the plants
on the deck to give way, the noife of
which founded fo difmal in the cabbin,
that I, who was at that time much
oppreffed with the fea-ficknefs, ima-
gined that the fate of our bark was
faft approaching.

22d. Still fqually and much rain.

23d. The dead-lights in; every
thing very wet from the quantity of
rain which had fallen, and myfelf
very fick.

24th. The weather moderate
throughout the 24 hours.—On this
day the fhip's company were put to
the

the allowance of *five* pints of water per day, as a neceffary precaution againft future accidents.

25th. Moderate and cloudy, with lightning to the Southward. On looking out for land, we faw Lord Howe's Ifland, a fmall fpot difcovered by Captain Wallis, and called, by the inhabitants of the Society Ifland, *Mopbea*; it lies in South latitude 16° 46″, and Weft longitude 154° 8″. At 5, P. M. we faw Mount *Lidgbird* S. E. by E. The Cutters were fent on fhore to feek for turtle; Lieutenant Ball having met with plenty when he firft difcovered this Ifland.

26th. We tacked the fhip to the Northward of Lord Howe's Ifland.

The

The Cutters returned without meeting with any fuccefs. There are goats, and a great number of brown birds about the fize of our crows : the noife made by this bird is loud and unpleafant, and when dreffed the flavour is ftrong and difagreeable.

27th. At 4 A. M we faw Mount *Gower*, diftance about 8 or 9 leagues N. N. E. from *Ball's Pyramid*. At 6 A. M. we difcovered Ring's Point. At noon we met with frefh breezes and fqually weather, which continued with little variation to the end of the month.

On the 1ft day of January, 1792, about midnight, a large Meteor was feen in the South-Weft quarter, which
took

took its courfe towards the North-
Weft. Until the 5th inftant, we had
moderate weather, which afforded me
the fatisfaction of partaking in the
chearful parties of thofe who were
within our wooden walls. Upon
looking out for land, we difcovered
the *Three Kings Head* Ifland off the
North end of New Zealand. At
4 we faw the Coaft of New Zealand.
At half paft 4, faw Cape Maria, at
which time Van Dieman's land bore
S. by W. and the North Cape S. E. by
E. diftant 7 or 8 leagues. It is remarkable that the land from Cape
Maria to the North Cape appears to
be defolate, barren, and rocky, without the leaft verdure or tree, excepting on the fummit of a hill over *Sandy
Bay*, where there appear *five* or *fix*.

6   CHAP.

CHAP. X.

The voyage continued—discover a num-
ber of Ice-islands—description of
them—singular story of a Shark—
with an anecdote relative thereto.

I Shall not here trouble my readers
with the regular dates and little varia-
tions customary in these distant latitudes; but simply notice the weather,
which was mostly fresh breezes, hazy,
and squally—splitting of sails, paf-
sing rock-weed, sea-weed, and such
like occurrences, met with by voyagers
in general.

On the 14th we saw several whales,
much rock-weed, and birds of different sorts.

I   16th.

16th. Cloudy, with a heavy fwell from N. E. Saw a number of filver birds.

17th. Obferved a curious porpoife, with a white bill and under-jaw, alfo a number of brown-winged birds around the fhip.

18th. Frefh gales and fqually; paffed a number of porpoifes.

19th. At 4 P. M. the wind fhifted fuddenly with a heavy fquall from N. N. E. to W. S. W. and continued fo the remainder of the night.

20th. The fame uncomfortable weather, with a long Wefterly fwell. Saw feveral whales. This weather
continued

continued with little variation during the remainder of the month.

The beginning of February, we had frequent fqualls and heavy feas, with rain, hail, and fleet.

On the 7th, we difcovered *Terra del Fuego*, and *York Minfter*, bearing N. E. by N. diftant about 7 or 8 leagues.

8th. Frefh breezes and hazy; York Minfter bore N. N. W. $\frac{1}{4}$ W. 8 or 9 leagues —In the afternoon of the fame day, the central Ifle of *Il de Fonzo* bore N. N. W. $\frac{3}{4}$ W. 8 or 9 leagues. At 4, land was feen at the maft-head, fuppofed to be the Ifland *Diego*. The extreme land to the N. W. $\frac{1}{2}$ W. was fuppofed to be *Cape*

Horn,

Horn, and that to the Eaftward *Barn-well Iflands.* At ½ paft 5, the land fuppofed *Cape Horn* bore W. N. W. 6 or 7 leagues.

The 12th was thick and foggy, with rain and frefh breezes. We faw albertroffes, penguins, and apparently fome land-birds fuppofed to come from Saint George's or Falkland Iflands.

14th. We had almoft a calm, faw fome land-birds, and caught one which was rather larger than a full-fized pigeon. Paffed Willis's Ifland, South Georgia, Eaft 125 leagues.

16th. Difcovered penguins and various other birds. The fea ran very high, and a hard gale ftruck the fhip violently.

17th. The

17th. The fame bluftering weather, with increafing gales. Saw feveral feals, penguins, and porpoifes, whales and fea-weed.

The enfuing morning, at 4 o'clock, feveral Ice-iflands appeared in fight. By the advice of Captain Parker I arofe to partake of this uncommon *fpectacle*. The courfe of one hour brought *feven* to our view, bearing E. by N. to N. N. W. diftance from the neareft *three* leagues. From this time until 10 o'clock feveral ice-iflands were feen. In order to fupport my drooping fpirits, I retired for a fhort time to ftrengthen my refolution, a precaution by no means unneceffary, as I could not help reflecting on the number of

I 3 navigators

navigators who had been arrefted and
frozen to death in the midft of thefe
tremendous maffes; it was in this
manner that the brave Sir Hugh Wil-
loughby was loft, with all his crew, in
1553, and in like manner Lord Mul-
grave in the year 1773 was caught in
the ice, and nearly experienced the
fame unhappy fate.

If it were poffible for voyagers to
diveft themfelves of the horror which
the eventful expectation of change
muft ever occafion; the view is at
once both beautiful and picturefque,
even to the moft incurious eye: the
forms affumed by the ice are extremely pleafing and grotefque; the water
which dafhes againft the ice freezes
into a variety of forms, and almoft
into

into every fhape which the imagina-
tion can frame.

The novelty of the fight engaged
the attention of every one on-board.
About 7 o'clock we beheld no lefs
than *fifteen* of thefe tremendous iflands
at one time, which obliged us to haul
our wind, and bear up frequently in
order to fail clear of them. Between
the hours of 8 and 10 we paffed *nine*
more, and at that time a large body
or field of ice appeared from North
to W. N. W. our diftance from it was
about 9 miles. We hauled our wind
to W. S. W. which courfe we ran for
feven or *eight* miles; the northernmoft
part of the field then bore N. N. E. $\frac{1}{2}$ E.
and the wefternmoft N. W. $\frac{1}{4}$ W. One
of the Iflands was 17$\frac{3}{4}$ miles in length,

I 4   and

and that on the fartheft extremity
was no lefs than $52\frac{1}{2}$ miles. At
meridian the neareft diftance was
about 6 miles.

On Sunday the 19th, the weather
was moderate and hazy. At noon
the dulnefs of the hemifphere, and
the fun appearing very faintly, made
many fuppofe land to be in fight; but,
on founding 120 fathom, no ground
was found: at 10 o'clock the fun
fhining bright, all parties were con-
vinced it was an ice-bank; this large
field or body, by the different bear-
ings, was thought to be near 18
miles in length, as appeared by the
diftance run by the log, and by the
workings of the different courfes that
the fhip had failed from 10 A. M. in
their

their laſt log until 5 P. M. in this, when the extremes of it bore Eaſt about 8 or 9 miles. At 6 o'clock the extremes of the ice in ſight bore S. E. $\frac{1}{2}$ S. diſtance 3 or 4 leagues. This moſt tremendous field made the twenty-ninth iſland of ice we had ſailed paſt, from 5 A. M. until 5 P. M. In the courſe of the day we diſcovered a number of birds, ſeals, and porpoiſes : the evening was very bluſtering, during the greater part of which the ſhip lay-to, and every one appeared anxious to know the event of this diſmal night.

On the 21ſt, we had a continuance of dark and diſmal weather, attended with heavy gales, inceſſant ſleet, and violent labourings of the ſhip.——Indeed,

deed all our little comforts were done
away by anxiety, fea-ficknefs, and
darknefs; the turbulent waves rendering it neceffary for the dead-lights to
be up on all fides; and the intenfe
cold obliged us to have ftoves and hot
fhot flung to heat the different cabins.

The 22nd. a great fwell remained
from the laft gale; the appearance of
ice was feen to windward again E. by
S. to N. E. by N. alfo whales, birds,
rock-weed, together with lightning
all round the compafs.

Thefe heavy feas and hard gales
were our chief attendants until the
27th, when the weather became more
moderate, and we once more began
to entertain the hope of revifiting
thofe friends, whom we had almoft

3   defpaired

defpaired of feeing again: but the anxiety of mind, which I had laboured under for fome time, would have been much more poignant had I not been participating the fate of fo many others whofe good example and patient refignation taught me to confider that I was but an infignificant individual amongft them.——Nay, had the danger been inevitable, it would have been fome confolation in approaching deftruction, to have had a profpect of fharing the fame fate with him whofe virtues I am left to bewail.

Hazy damp weather continued during the firft part of the month of March. We difcovered frequent fhoals of porpoifes, alfo Cape hens, al-

albertroffes, and other birds. Singular as the circumftance may at firft
appear, a large fhark was caught, on
opening of which an old Prayer-book,
now in my poffeffion, was taken out
of its belly ; thofe who know the
ravenous appetite of this rapacious
fifh, will not be furprifed at the ex-
planation——as there was a marine
on-board whofe name was written
in it, but who probably from fear of
punifhment denied that it was his. It
appears to have belonged formerly to
a convict, as on one of the leaves was
written " TO DIE," and underneath
" REPRIEVED," with a fpace left on
purpofe to infert the day of the month.
The above circumftance is probably
unique. It was wittily obferved, on
the occafion, that it would not have
been

been fo aftonifhing if a *Law*-book had been found inftead of a *Prayer*-book, —as the fhark was always thought more of the *Lawyer* than the *Parfon*, being called by failors a *Sea-Law-yer*; as the following little anecdote, related to me upon this occafion, will fully evince.

A certain Judge, on his paffage to the Eaft-Indies, looking in diftant amaze at the flouncing of an enormous fhark, upon which the failors were operating, enquired with retiring trepidation, "what the prodigious " creature could poffibly be?" " *No-* " *thing*," replied a Tar, in a tone of voice better conceived than expreffed, —" *Nothing, your Honour, but a* " *Sea-Lawyer*."

The

The profpe&t now began to brighten ; the expe&ation of returning fafe to the Cape, revived our drooping fpirits. Dinner-parties, cards, &c. were once more the paftime of thofe on-board : even our little birds and plants appeared fenfible of the return of funfhine and tranquillity.

CHAP.

CHAP. XI.

Arrive at Table-Bay—take up our abode at Mr. Peter de Witt's—mild treatment of the Slaves at the Cape—a Gentoo—a visit to Constantia—return to Cape Town.

ON the 12th of March, land was once more in view, and at 6 o'clock in the evening the ship was running into *Table-Bay*, where we found two Dutch frigates, a brig of war, several Dutch Indiamen, and ships of different nations. We saw no one from shore that night. Happy at our safe arrival after so many anxieties, the remainder of the evening passed away

very

very agreeably, and the next morning
at an early hour one of our officers
went on-fhore, and returned, accompanied by Mr. Peter de Witt, with
frefh butter, lemons, grapes, figs,
apples, meat, and vegetables; refrefhments which we began to ftand in
need of; for, although we did not ab-
folutely want provifions, our ftores in
general were nearly exhaufted; the
fheep we took from this place had loft
fo much that the whole quarter when
boiled has not been larger than a fore
quarter of lamb.

When we formerly landed at the
Cape, my readers will remember, that
we lodged at Mrs. de Witt's. We now
took our abode at the houfe of Mr.
Peter de Witt's, a fon of the good
lady

lady above-mentioned. Colonel and Mrs. Gordon loſt no time in paying their congratulations upon our return, and renewing their friendly invitations; as did alſo the Governor, whoſe name was Monſieur Renies. The Colonel was ſo obliging as to ſend his carriage for me ; and on my arrival at his villa I had the pleaſure of finding all our marine officers, and ſuch of our gentlemen as could be ſpared from the ſhip; for, although ſafely landed in this healthful and plentiful country, we all had ſufficient reaſons for wiſhing to proceed on our voyage.

We found the family in good health, nor was their polite attention in the leaſt diminiſhed; nay, after our being confined on-board for three

K   months,

months, even the villa itſelf appeared,
if poſſible, more beautiful than before.

The lady of Mr. de Witt was extremely attentive to us, and endea-
voured to render our abode as comfortable as poſſible. According to
the beſt of my recollection there were
thirty ſlaves belonging to this houſe.

The beauty of one of the females
particularly ſtruck my attention; the
elegance of her deportment, the ſym-
metry of her features, and the pleaſing
curl of her fine dark hair, could not
paſs unnoticed by any, excepting
thoſe who were unwilling to pay
that tribute to the ſimplicity of nature, which all the aſſiſtance of art
could not place them in the poſſeſ-
ſion of.

With

With fatisfaction I noticed that the
flaves were treated at the Cape with
the greateft humanity: and only in
name bore the degrading diftinction.

They are let out by the month,
week, or day, during which time
they are obliged to earn for their
mafters a certain fixed fum. The
male flaves wear their own hair, upon
which they fet a great value, wrapped
up in a handkerchief, fomewhat like
a turban; the females wreath up
theirs, and fix it on their heads with
a large pin. Trowfers conftitute the
other part of their drefs; and as a
token of their fervile condition, they
always go barefooted, and without a
hat.

K 2   Pre-

Previous to fitting down to meals, it is the cuftom of the Cape for a female flave to bring a bafon and a towel for the company to wafh their hands ; which is repeated on rifing from table. In the houfes of the wealthy, every one of the company has a flave behind his chair to wait upon him : this flave has frequently a large palm-leaf in his hand, by way of a fan to drive away the flies, which are extremely troublefome in thefe climates.

The company's gardens, at a fmall diftance from Cape Town, are very pleafant, and the chief refort of perfons of refpectability in that country. Mrs. Gordon has frequently called upon me in her carriage, and obliged me me with a ride to fee them; and nothing could be more refreshing than the fragrant evening breezes that generally prevail in thefe hot climates.

Our time was now taken up in vifiting and receiving vifits; we had feveral invitations from the Governor, where the entertainments were elegant, and the company numerous, confifting chiefly of marine officers, and thofe belonging to our fhip.

On the 18th, a Dutch Indiaman arrived from Batavia, and fhortly after we were gratified with the company of Captain Edwards, of his Majefty's fhip the Pandora, who a few days after landing embarked, and afterwards purfued his voyage in our fhip:

K 3   the

the convicts alfo who had efcaped
from Port Jackfon were taken up at
fea by the Pandora, and returned
to England in the Gorgon.

About this time I had the pleafure
of receiving a vifit from Mrs. Johnfon,
a lady who had arrived at the Cape
on her return from the Eaft Indies.
I was alfo introduced, by Colonel
Burrington, to the acquaintance of a
lady, who was fo obliging as to favour me with the fight of a Gentoo,
which is indeed fingular in every refpect; they having a gold ring upon
almoft every toe, alfo in their ears
and nofes, and large filver rings round
the ancles; they wear the hair faftened with a filver pin and a curious
piece of India muflin, which negligent-
ly,

ly, though not inelegantly, almoft covers their bodies.

A party of us had fixed a day for a jaunt to Conftantia, a little diftrict at the Cape of Good Hope, confifting of two farms, which produce the well-known wine fo much prized in Europe. It is fituated at the diftance of a mile and a half from *Alphen*, in a bending, formed by and nearly under the ridge of hills, which comes from Muyfen-Mountain, and juft where it ftrikes off towards *Houtbay*. One of thefe farms is called Little Conftantia: here the white wine is made; the other produces the red.

On the morning of the day appointed we fet out in two carriages,

K 4   each

each containing four perfons, and the
gentlemen on horfeback. We had rode
but a very little way before we were
overtaken by a fmart fhower of rain;
and as the front feats of the vehicle
were not fheltered from it, we were
fprinkled in a fhort time to fuch a degree that, when we arrived at the end
of our journey, we found ourfelves
neceffitated to refer for a change of
cloathing to the good people of the
houfe, who willingly granted our requeft although we were entire ftrangers to them.

We met here the Governor of Cape
Town, with fome captains and offi-
cers belonging to the Dutch Man of
War then lying at Table-Bay. It
being the ufual compliment in that
Country

Country for the Lady of the houfe to refign her feat at the table, I was invefted with that honour, and accordingly placed at the head of a numerous party, (moftly ftrangers,) deprived of all the decorations which vanity, a few hours before, had induced me to beftow upon myfelf; for, my coat and hat being wet through, I was furnifhed with a large white jacket belonging to the lady of the houfe, one half of which I could have fpared with great convenience.

We were received and entertained with attention and refpect, and tafted the different forts of the famous wine which borrows its name from the fpot where the grapes grow; although I think I have eaten a fimilar grape

in

in the Mediterranean; which conjecture is in fome meafure confirmed by the great quantity of wine that appears under this name;—if I am wrong in my fufpicions, thefe fmall vineyards muft afford a profufion indeed!

The weather continued much the fame during the remainder of the day; however, as we were none of us ftrangers to a watery element, it rendered it lefs troublefome to all, and we returned in our borrowed garbs to Cape Town, well pleafed with our vifit; and affording no fmall amufement to our friends, from the laughable appearance which we made.

This excurfion ferved us frequently for converfation, and was nearly the laft we took during our ftay.

CHAP.

CHAP. XII.

*Some account of Cape Town—departure
from the Cape—Afcenfion Road—
the voyage continued—reach Saint
Helens—land at Portfmouth—arrive in London—Conclufion.*

ON our return to the Cape, I took
feveral opportunities of walking about
the town, in which there are many
excellent gardens laid out in the neat-
eft tafte, and producing fruit and
culinary vegetables in great abundance.

The extenfive and beautiful garden belonging to the Company is

3   always

always open to the publick ; and it is from this garden that the ſtranger, on his arrival, meets with his firſt refreſhments.

The town is adorned with three large ſquares, in one of which ſtands the Proteſtant church; it likewiſe has a fountain in it, which furniſhes the inhabitants with water. In the other is the Town-hall. The third is laid out for the convenience of the country people, who bring their goods to market.

While I was paſſing my time thus agreeably at the Cape, Captain Parker and the officers were more eſſentially employed in the neceſſary preparations both for our ſafety and ſupport.

port. The Governor and Colonel Gordon's family feemed to ftudy what prefents might be moft acceptable for us when we next embarked; owing to their goodnefs, we added, to our ftores, wine, goats, liquors, and many other refrefhments which were likely to be ferviceable to us.

The Oftrich feather is one of the moft gaudy and valuable purchafes that can be made in this country; and, to thofe who are amateurs of birds, I can, from experience, recommend the Cape Canary; the plumage of which is much like our green linnet, the breaft more yellow, and the colour, if any thing, more lively; it has a very pretty note, and, what renders it ftill more agreeable, is its being rather louder,

louder, though fimilar to that general favourite and winter companion, the fprightly Robin. One morning I purchafed *fixteen*, and the cage containing them, for the moderate fum of *four* fhillings and *fix* pence.

On the 31ft, we took our final dinner at the hofpitable villa before mentioned, and reluctantly bade adieu to the good Colonel and his lady, whofe attention to ftrangers I have fignified in the former part of this narrative.

The laft farewel being taken, accompanied by a confiderable number of our friends, we once more repaired on-board, after having paffed a month at the Cape with much fatisfaction and

and pleaſure. I began now to turn my thoughts towards Old England, and encouraged the pleaſing expectation of being ſhortly in the company of a mother and two dear children, from whom I had been ſo long abſent.

Our birds, &c. being replaced and laſhed as before, we ſet ſail on the 6th of April. With moderate weather we continued our voyage to Saint Helena, which Iſland was firſt ſeen on the 18th at midnight, and by $\frac{1}{2}$ paſt 7 in the morning we could perceive three ſhips in the road, viz. 1 Swediſh, 1 Engliſh Indiaman, and a Whaler. The neceſſity of returning with the diſpatches of the Colony as ſpeedily as poſſible left us no time for delay at this iſland; we therefore contented

contented ourfelves with viewing the fhore at a confiderable diftance; thus, favoured with pleafant breezes and trade-winds, we rolled merrily on till the 23d, when we anchored in 15 fathom, at *Afcenfion Road*. At this uninhabited Ifland we found the *Betfy*, an American fchooner, with the mafter, his wife, and four or five men on-board, without a grain of tea or fcarcely any provifions. Our boats were fent on-fhore, with men, to try if it were poffible to procure fome turtle; they fhortly returned with a fufficient quantity, which was of in-finite fervice to numbers on-board.

The fea continued tranquil and the fhip ftill, which made our fhort ftay very agreeable. After leaving the body

bodyof a child on shore for inter-
ment, we again set sail on the 25th.

The moderate weather, and fine
trade-winds, added to the pleasing
hope of seeing our friends in a little
time, made the remainder of our
voyage appear short. The beginning
of the month of May, we had light
winds and frequent calms, which
tended to prolong our journey, and
to do away the expectations we had
formed of returning to Spithead about
the 6th of June.

However, the intrusion of calms
was easily endured by us; for, after sail-
ing so many thousand miles together,
our little parties were, if possible, more
agreeable than at first setting-out,

L   and

and for this reason it muſt not be ſup-
poſed that our friendſhip for each
other had in the leaſt degree diminiſhed, but much the contrary.

About the middle of June, we
reached Saint Helens : Captain Parker and the other gentlemen, intruſted
with government diſpatches, fixed the
ſame evening for their departure for
London. Captain Edwards accompanied me on-ſhore, and after four
hours rowing againſt wind and tide,
we landed at the *Salley Port*, at Portſ-
mouth, where we were met by many,
who, aſtoniſhed at the ſpeedy return
of our ſhip, cheerfully congratulated
us on our arrival.

We

We repaired to the Fountain Inn, and, after feeing the above gentlemen fet off for London, I retired to reft. Early the next morning, accompanied by one of our officers, I took chaife, and arrived in town at 8 o'clock the fame evening, where I had the happinefs of again embracing an affectionate mother, and a little daughter, who is at this prefent time one of my greateft comforts; my other child, a boy, had died during my abfence. This vacancy in my family did not, however, remain long after my arrival; for, on the Thurfday *following*, Captain Parker had luckily taken lodgings in Frith-ftreet, Soho, *in the morning*, where, after a fhort ride from my friend's houfe, I was fafe in bed at

L 2   4 o'clock

4 o'clock in the afternoon. This little boy is of the number of thofe for whofe *benefit*, by the advice of my friends, I have taken the liberty to fet forth this narrative ; humbly hoping that my kind readers will pafs over the many faults with which it abounds, when they reflect that it was written under the preffure of mind, occafioned by the unexpected lofs of him, who was indeed an indulgent hufband, and a tender parent. The youngeft of thefe fatherlefs children is an infant of *feven* months, who has chiefly been on my left arm, whilft the right was employed in bringing once more to my recollection the pleafing occurrences of *fifteen* months, fpent in the company of *him*, whofe kind attention fupported me under all my affliction:—

7   but

but the fcene is changed—a retrofpect of the *paſt* tends only to augment my *prefent* calamities ; whilſt the *future* prefents nothing to my view but the gloomy profpect of additional misfortunes and additional forrows !

F I N I S.

For EU product safety concerns, contact us at Calle de José Abascal, 56–1°,
28003 Madrid, Spain or eugpsr@cambridge.org.